MW00613967

Transformational
LEADERSHIP

"Randy Dobbs is a leader with a big heart and an eye to the future, a strong leader among peers. Dobbs believes in teamwork, best practice sharing, communication and leading by example. He clearly draws out the best in others from the level of field engineers to business executives in order to help drive change to create an extremely successful global service business. As a peer and a friend, **I highly recommend learning from Randy's life experiences in this book.**"

—Dan Slater, Global Service VP, Optos Inc.

"It's all about communications. Randy's key ingredient for achieving transformational leadership is his ability to communicate. Whether it is his ability to share his vision, mobilize employee commitment, or coach his team to higher levels of performance, **Randy delivers his message to every part of the organization in a way that "keeps it real."** Part showman, part change evangelist…he is an inspirational leader!"

—Karen Query, former GE & GE Capital HR Executive
and currently President of her own HR Consulting firm

"Dobbs and I clicked the first time we met at a retreat in our Philips Medical Systems days. His secret sauce approach to change at Philips was responsible for completely transforming that organization and along with it my career. **My application of Dobbs' method continues to pay huge dividends** as my career moves forward."

—Bill Mixon, President and CEO of USIS,
a leading global security services provider

"When I think of Randy, passion comes to the forefront. In the early 90's, we were transforming the Service business from a reactive "fix it when it is broken" approach to a process focused, proactive business model that put the customer and GE on the same side. Randy, who was leading the SE Region, led the transformation by eliminating an organizational layer while driving the Local Customer Team concept. With a hands-on, passionate approach, **he demonstrated it was possible to improve operating efficiency, customer satisfaction and employee ownership—all at the same time.**"

—Tom Dunham, former VP & General Manager
America's Service, GE Medical Systems

"After observing Dobbs' leadership skills and the rapid implementation of highly effective operational processes at USIS—which drove results and improvements beyond our expectations—my team was so impressed that we engaged Randy as a Senior Operating Executive in our firm. **I recommend his book without hesitation.**"

—Pat Welsh, Founding Partner, Welsh, Carson, Anderson
& Stowe, a private equity firm that manages total capital
of $20 billion and has invested in over 170 companies and
financed over 650 follow-on acquisitions.

"As a long-standing investment banking advisor to USIS, I had the opportunity to witness the company's performance over many years. In the face of some unpredictable and difficult challenges, Randy's operational expertise, hands-on leadership, and strategic vision were the keys to transforming the operational and financial success of the company. **Randy is the quintessential change agent.**"

—David Baron, Head of Financial Sponsors Advisory,
Macquarie Capital (USA) Inc.

Transformational
LEADERSHIP

A BLUEPRINT FOR REAL ORGANIZATIONAL CHANGE

Randy Dobbs

WITH PAUL ROBERT WALKER

Parkhurst Brothers, Inc., Publishers
LITTLE ROCK

PARKHURST BROTHERS, INC., PUBLISHERS

www.pbros.net

Parkhurst Brothers books are distributed to the trade through the Chicago Distribution Center, a unit of the University of Chicago Press, and may be ordered through Ingram Book Company, Baker & Taylor, Follett Library Resources and other book industry wholesalers. To order from the University of Chicago's Chicago Distribution Center, phone 1-800-621-2736 or send a fax to 1-800-621-8476. Copies of this and other Parkhurst Brothers, Inc., Publishers titles are available to organizations and corporations for purchase in quantity by contacting Special Sales Department at our home office location, listed on our website.

Printed in the United States of America

First Edition 2010

2010 2011 2012 2013 2014 2015 2016 2017 2018   18 17 16 15 14 13 12 11 10 9 8 7 6 5 4 3 2 1

Library of Congress Control Number: 2009942595

ISBN: Hardcover 978-1-935166-19-1   [10 digit: 1-935166-19-0]

This book is printed on archival-quality paper that meets requirements of the American National Standard for Information Sciences, Permanence of Paper, Printed Library Materials, ANSI Z39.48-1984.

Design Director and Dustjacket/cover design:
Wendell E. Hall

Page design:
Shelly Culbertson

Acquired for Parkhurst Brothers, Inc., Publishers by:
Ted Parkhurst

Editor:
Roger Armbrust

Proofreaders:
Bill and Barbara Paddack

DISCOUNTS FOR BULK PURCHASE: Institutions, schools, and organizations may purchase this title in bulk at substantial savings off the suggested list price. Please email randy@pbros.net or refer to our website **www.pbros.net** for current contact information from our Special Sales Department.

Dedication

To my grandmother, Elizabeth Young Johnson,

who taught me the value of hard work,

to never give up, and to understand that every

challenge is just another opportunity.

Acknowledgments

A great many people in my life have assisted me in my personal and professional growth, and are a big part of the story and lessons presented in this book. I wish to thank them all, but there are far too many to name personally, so I would like to give special thanks to the following... to my family: Joel, Elizabeth, and Judy Dobbs; to a short list of GE leaders who had such an impact on my professional life: Bill Fenoglio, Jim Bennett, Bob Etien, Guy Rhodes, Jim DelMauro, Tom Dunham, and Jack Welch; to Jouko Karvinen and the Philips Medical Systems leadership team for giving me the opportunity to succeed and grow outside of the GE system; to the entire team at Welsh, Carson, Anderson & Stowe, especially Pat Welsh and John Clark, for providing me the opportunity to drive success at USIS; and last but certainly not least, to just a few of my colleagues who served on one or more of my leadership teams, many of whom shared their experiences in this book: John Moore, Karen Query, Bill Mixon, Dave Kaminsky, James Choi, Ron Hancock, Mike Santelli, Susan Parent, and Robert Calamia.

I would also like to thank the key players who helped bring this book from idea to publication: Paul Robert Walker, my close friend and writing partner, who helped me not just to think about this book but about my life; Al Zuckerman of Writers House, who gave us valuable feedback in the early stages of the project; and Ted Parkhurst and Roger Armbrust of Parkhurst Brothers, who enthusiastically embraced the book and brought it to publication.

Table of Contents

What is Transformational Leadership?

Do you know how to double a privately held company's earnings in 36 months? Do you know how to reduce a workforce of 5,700 to less than 3,100 in 18 months and have the remaining employees feel good about it? Do you know how to analyze a business losing $100 million a year and move it to profitability in two years? Do you know how to take 7,000 nationally distributed employees and get them on the same page regarding business objectives and policies?

No simple answers exist to these questions. I know from personal experience, because I confronted these complex business challenges and achieved success in all of them. However, one simple phrase drove my success and can drive your success: transformational leadership.

I know you're thinking—here's another book on buzzwords—and I'm the last guy who's going to throw buzzwords at you. But I will tell you this: You can only address, change or improve tough business issues through my one buzzphrase: transformational leadership.

There are many kinds of leaders, and far too many leaders are caretakers. They keep the business running; perhaps they even improve performance a little by being good caretakers, but they do not fundamentally change the business. They do not leave the business exponentially better than when they arrived. You can achieve that kind of change only through transformational leadership.

What is transformational leadership? Everybody has an opinion, but after more than 30 years of achieving real business transformation, I clearly see that it involves five key skill sets:

1. **Build a culture...**Every business has a culture, whether the people in that business know it or not. A transformational leader must recognize the business's current culture and work to make it a better, stronger culture that fits the people in the business, the nature of the business, and the customers the business serves. There is no one right culture—it depends on the situation—but one of the most fundamental tasks of a great leader is to transform the culture.

2. **Improve esprit de corps...**We often talk about employee morale in the business world, but I prefer to think of it as esprit de corps—a French term that literally means "spirit of the body," but refers to the spirit of a group as a single body. This means that everyone in the organization shares the same vision, and feels enthusiastic about being part of that vision and working together toward clearly defined collective goals. In simple terms: Once you establish a culture, you must establish esprit de corps so the people in the organization will buy into that culture.

3. **Communicate issues and actions...**Every great leader is a great communicator. No organization can follow your lead unless all its members understand where you are leading them and why it's in their best interests to follow you. Clear, consistent, and comprehensive communication represents the single-most powerful tool for a transformational leader.

4. **Change the financial results...**Let's be honest: Businesses exist to earn money for the investors, shareholders, and other stakeholders, including employees. A successful business not only offers a substantial return on investment, but also has the capability of offering higher salaries and better benefits for its employees. Therefore, the simplest and clearest measure of a transformational leader is the ability to improve financial results. Even if you improve the culture, the esprit de corps, and the communication, you have not transformed the business until you transform the financial results.

5. **Leave behind a cadre of future transformational leaders...** No leader stays in the same leadership role forever. In fact, many transformational leaders move on to other challenges on a regular basis. A transformational leader's final, most lasting mark is that the transformation doesn't stop when he or she leaves the business. A truly successful transformation proves self-sustaining through a cadre of transformational leaders, trained and mentored by the original leader, who are ready to take the reins and continue the ongoing process of business transformation.

Sounds exciting, doesn't it? I can assure you that no better feeling exists in the business world than truly transforming a company. It's like being an artist in a business suit—a reason to get up early and work late, a purpose that makes your job a joy. Those possessing this ability can call their shots and command higher compensation.

So how do you do it? How do you stop being a caretaker and become a transformational leader? I believe this requires a continual transformation within yourself, and that can only come from paying thoughtful attention and learning from your experiences.

Sounds easy, but it isn't. Transformation requires a level of discipline and self-awareness unavailable to just anyone. Do you have it? If you're reading this introduction, I bet you do.

I don't believe I learned transformational leadership at the small state university I attended any more than students learn it in an Ivy League school. My own talent for leadership results from my family influences, good and bad, my failures and learning from those failures, and my continual experimentation in each new transformational opportunity. You have your own influences, your own failures, your own experimentations. The key is what you learn from them and how you use them to transform yourself and the organizations you lead.

The lessons I offer were not gained through one experience but many; not just through my own experiences, but the experiences of many mentors including a great woman—my grandmother, Elizabeth Young—whom I will discuss further in the book. She, like many others, taught me that transformational leadership has no gender, age, race, color, or ethnicity...no limitations at all.

It's like riding the power of the wind: The power is there for all, but only a few catch it and ride it where they want to go. After reading this book, considering these lessons, and applying them to your own experiences and your own career, I believe you will become one of the few.

Enjoy the ride!

CORE VALUES

CHAPTER 1

Who Am I, Anyway?

When embarking on a journey into uncharted territory, you want to know about the guide. The same goes for this journey into the world of transformational leadership. Who is Randy Dobbs, anyway? And why should you listen to what I have to say?

The short answer is...I'm a guy who never quit in 59 years, no matter what obstacles I faced, and I've faced more than my fair share of them! I grew up in a small southern town, where I was fortunate to have a very special person in my early life—my grandmother—who taught me life lessons through words and examples that made me an exceptionally strong person. That's the good news.

The bad news is that I needed every ounce of that strength to face what life dealt me after my family left that town: a broken home, an abusive-alcoholic stepfather, and a suicidal mother. I graduated high school as an honors student despite a home atmosphere of violence and chaos; and I put myself through a local state university working full-time in a machine shop, sleeping four hours a night and existing on peanut-butter sandwiches. I still keep my machinists' union card to remind me of those days and just in case I ever need a job. At this point in my life, I doubt I'll need that, but it's nice to know it's there.

Considering where I came from, I could have easily slipped through the cracks and become a lost soul...an alcoholic, a drug addict...or just a nondescript survivor. Instead, I found a level of success in the business world that would seem unimaginable for a guy with my background. If I can do it, you can do it, too!

As I write this, I recently completed my third assignment as a CEO—for USIS, the largest provider of background investigations to the federal government, a top provider of background screenings to commercial industry, and one of the most significant providers of highly skilled, cleared personnel supporting the national security mission in countries around the world, including Iraq, Afghanistan, and Indonesia. During my 3½-year tenure at USIS, I grew revenue by 18%, grew earnings by 70%, turned around a serious employee-morale problem, introduced new technology tools and operational efficiencies, and orchestrated two major value-added acquisitions and the company's sale to a private equity firm.

Before my USIS assignment, I served as CEO of Philips Medical Systems North America, where I transformed four standalone acquisitions purchased for more than $5 billon into one integrated business. This included a major restructuring within my first 90 days to eliminate some 250 management positions and create a new senior leadership team gleaned from inside and outside the Philips structure. Focusing on accountability and execution from both a leadership and process perspective, we significantly moved the business performance needle over a two-year period, including revenue growth of 12%, operational income growth of more than 30%, and improved cash flow, while lowering inventory levels by more than a third and gaining market share with an excited, focused, and committed workforce.

The heart of my career involved more than 25 years with the General Electric organization. I rose from an hourly worker on a summer job to become a corporate officer and CEO of GE Capital IT Solutions—where I won the Turnaround Business of the Year Award in 2002.

I am proud to consider myself a protégé of Jack Welch, who recognized and encouraged my leadership potential, but my relationship with Jack was only the tip of the iceberg in my GE experience. I held just about every kind of position you can imagine, from working in an assembly-line paint booth to managing a whole production unit of line workers; from making sales calls on customers who didn't want to see me to developing marketing plans for a product that faced serious market challenges; from reengineering a plant in America's heartland to managing a new, ground-breaking plant in Mexico.

Although I moved steadily up through the GE world and into new opportunities at Philips and USIS, I faced resistance every step of the way: resistance to me as a Southerner from a small state college in a world of Ivy League graduates; resistance to me as a guy with new ideas that challenged the status quo and sometimes challenged the bottom line; resistance created by my own failings and misjudgments. I have a proven gift for business leadership, but I have made plenty of mistakes along the way—everyone does. The not-so-secret key to success in business, and anything else life has to offer, is the ability to view every setback as an opportunity rather than a defeat. I credit my grandmother with teaching me that way of thinking.

I thought a lot about how to begin these lessons on transformational leadership. It's a complex subject, and many talents, experiences, and commitments go into being a true transformational leader. However, the more I thought about it, the more I considered my own experiences and talked with my friends and business associates, one thing became clear: The fundamental lesson for any transformational leader—the lesson that everything else is built upon—is that you will encounter resistance to your efforts and must **never give up.** Or as I like to put it: "If You Want to Win, You Can't Quit."

CHAPTER 2

If You Want to Win, You Can't Quit

After I became a GE corporate officer in 1997, Jack Welch invited me to lunch, along with a couple of other new officers, and presented each of us with a silver money clip engraved with our initials. As he handed me the money clip, he said, "Congratulations, Randy. May it always be full." It was a nice personal touch—the kind that made Jack such a strong leader of other leaders.

That was a great day for me but only the beginning of the story. I have two of those money clips, because I am one of only two leaders during Jack Welch's tenure as GE CEO to become a corporate officer, lose my stripes, and earn them again. That never-quit attitude forms the heart of this first lesson on transformational leadership. And this lesson, as well as many others, begins with my grandmother, Elizabeth Young.

I began a sort of apprenticeship with my grandmother when I was six years old, a big brother with three younger sisters. The youngest was born with brittle bones, spending her earliest years in and out of hospitals, suffering more than 30 fractures by the time she was two. My mother had all she could handle taking care of her. So I and my next youngest sister lived with my grandmother in a big, beautiful white house—think *Gone with the Wind* on a smaller scale—just down the street from Auburn University in Auburn, Alabama. My other sister lived with my father and mother in our modest family home across town.

I don't know why we were divided up as we were, but I was over-joyed because I adored my grandmother. Elizabeth Young was a tall woman for her generation, with a commanding presence and charisma. She was fun to be around but no-nonsense when it came to teaching me right and wrong. Most important, she had a remarkable commitment to the challenges of being a leader.

At the time I lived with her in the big white house, my grandmother ran a laundry across the street...not a storefront laundry service where you drop off your clothes, but a full-scale laundry and dry-cleaning plant with about 75 employees and a fleet of delivery trucks. Elizabeth's father, my great-grandfather, founded the business and died of a heart attack from the stress of trying to keep it afloat during the Great Depression.

That was 1934, and my grandmother was living in California with my grandfather and their two-year-old daughter Betty, my mother. Elizabeth never liked California—she was a Southern woman who loved the South—and she told my grandfather she was going home to help her family. She was taking Betty with her, and he could come with them or stay. He decided to stay, and they later divorced.

That was an amazingly strong and independent-minded decision for a woman with a two-year-old child in 1934. My grandfather was an attorney, a good breadwinner, but she turned her back on that life to help her family. She became a single mother, a businesswoman, and the breadwinner for her own family, which included herself, her daughter, and her widowed mother. Elizabeth was the oldest sibling, and she felt an obligation to support her mother in the house where they had all grown up.

My grandmother later told a local historian that they had to make arrangements with all of her father's creditors to keep the laundry running. "It took us ten years to pay it all off," she said, "but we paid it off and owned it free and clear." That was the sense of commitment and refusal to quit that she passed on to me.

I didn't know this history when I was six years old, but every day I saw a woman who never wavered in her commitment to her work and to providing for her family. By that time, "her family" included not only herself and her mother, but my immediate family, too. My father worked for my grandmother, managing the delivery fleet; and my grandmother gave us additional support that allowed us to live on a higher level than we could afford on my father's salary. That led to problems later on, but she did it out of love and because she had a gift for running a business. Some families have a patriarch who plays that kind of role; we had a matriarch.

My grandmother was in her early 50s at the time I lived with her. She was the first one at that laundry every morning before sunrise, and the last one to leave long after sundown. I could see her exhaustion every night at the dinner table; but she never took a day off, just kept getting up in the morning and doing her job. I lived with her for three years, and she taught me many lessons during that time. This was the most basic one: Keep on keeping on, never give up, don't accept quitting as an option.

I don't think she actually said that to me at that time—although she did later when I needed to hear it—but she *showed* me, and it made an enormous impression on me as a young boy. It gave me an inner strength that enabled me to get through some very tough times in my personal life and in the business world. I'd like to share a few of those experiences.

✳ ✳ ✳ ✳

My parents divorced when I was thirteen. We lived in Memphis at that time, and my mother married a truck driver named Bernie, from Jonesboro, Arkansas. We moved to Jonesboro during my freshman year in high school, and I was a sophomore when Bernie showed his true colors as an abusive alcoholic who spent his money on drinking, gambling, and fast cars.

He'd take his paycheck on Fridays and go blow it at the dog track in West Memphis, on the Arkansas side of the Mississippi. If he had a bad day, he'd come home in an alcoholic rage and take it out on my mother and the kids. I remember one time my mom had made a chocolate cake. When Bernie discovered it was made out of ingredients in a box instead of being made from scratch, he tossed it right out the door. If there wasn't enough grease in the green beans, he'd fling them across the floor.

Throwing food was bad enough, but it got worse. He came home one night and started beating my mother. I stood between them and he beat up on me. I was tall, about 6'5" by that time, but I was a gangly 15-year-old kid, who had never been in a fight in my life. Bernie was over six feet himself, powerfully built, a tough truck driver with an intimidating, violent personality. My sisters were in hysterics, so after getting pounded by Bernie, I grabbed them and left the house, walking down the country road until I found a haven with one of Bernie's uncles. He took us in and kept us safe until the situation calmed down at our house.

Like a lot of abused women, my mother became deeply depressed. One night, when Bernie was away, she called me into her room. She was lying on the bed in the dark. "Randy," she said, "I want you to always take care of your sisters."

"Why are you telling me this, Mom?" I asked.

She told me she had overdosed on sleeping pills and was lying down to die. "You can't die, Mom," I said. "I need you, and the girls need you." Then I called an ambulance, and they took her to the hospital to pump her stomach. She tried it again within a year.

My grandmother came to visit after my mother's second overdose. I don't know what Elizabeth said to Betty, but she must have talked some sense into her, because there were no more suicide attempts. I was over-joyed to see my grandmother, of course, and I will never forget what she said to me at that time:

"I know it's difficult for you, Randy, but you can't ever give up. You come from special people who worked hard to succeed no matter how difficult the situation was. Remember who you are and be strong. Never, ever, give up." I took that as my motto then, and I still follow that motto every day in the business world.

Unfortunately, even a woman as strong as my grandmother couldn't change Bernie, and our life continued to be punctuated by bizarre, violent episodes. It seemed like every other weekend he would get drunk and do something crazy and mean. One of his craziest episodes came when I insisted on playing basketball my senior year. It's a story that clearly exemplifies the distorted world I lived in.

✳ ✳ ✳ ✳

My mother and Bernie were seldom supportive of anything "extra" that I wanted to do, but in my junior year they let me play both football and basketball. That was a big deal. I wasn't a great player, but I made the varsity football team as a punter and played on the junior-varsity basket-ball team. That summer, I asked for a basketball goal for my birthday, with a concrete pad so I could practice my shooting and dribbling. That was one of Bernie's sober periods, and he and my mother actually gave me what I asked for—one of the few happy times I had in that house.

I worked at a local bait shop that summer, opening the store at 4 A.M., selling night crawlers, minnows, and shotgun shells. By the end of summer, I had saved about $500, which would pay for all the things I needed my senior year: clothes, books, and anything "extra." Then I did something stupid—took my mother's car out on the road one Sunday, driving too fast, ran off into a ditch and smashed the right fender. Bernie took every dollar I had to pay for fixing it. My $500 went a long way in those days—you could buy a brand new car for $2,500—and I suspect my lost savings was more than enough to cover the damage. But it didn't end there.

Bernie decided that I shouldn't be playing sports after school, that I should get a job instead. I already had the bait-shop job during summers and on weekends, and I'd worked hard to prepare for the football season; so I told him I was going to play anyway. He said that he and my mother would not pay for anything I needed, and they wouldn't help me with rides home after practice. I'd have to figure everything out myself. I didn't say anything, but I thought, *Fuck you, Bernie!* I bummed rides with friends who were on the team and had a successful season. I was co-captain and ultimately played three positions—punter, defensive back, and center—so I was in on every play.

Bernie didn't like the fact that I was playing football, but he let me slide as long as I didn't ask for anything. When basketball season began, I needed a new pair of shoes, because the ones I wore my junior year were completely worn out. Naturally, Bernie refused to buy me the shoes and forced my mother to go along with him. "You played football," he said. "You made your choice and that's it." My father was paying them $50 per child each month for child support, a lot of money in those days; but they refused to buy me a pair of basketball shoes. This was 1967, when a pair of high-topped Converse All Stars cost about $15.

I was completely broke. I didn't have money for clothes, let alone basketball shoes. I had two shirts, two pairs of jeans, and one pair of penny loafers. That was it. I wore a different shirt every other day. I wasn't going to let any of that stop me from playing basketball. I played the whole season with a pair of shoes I borrowed from my coach, still bumming rides from my friends.

One Friday night, about a week into the season, Bernie came home drunk and drove his Ford Ranchero up against the pole of the basketball goal outside our house. He destroyed his bumper as he rammed the pole again and again until it broke and fell to the ground. Then he went and got a can of gasoline he used for the lawn mower, poured it all over the broken basketball goal, and set it on fire. Lit by the flames, he turned to me with a drunken gleam in his eye and snarled, "Now play basketball."

As I watched the whole bizarre scene, I realized that Bernie was more than abusive; he was psychotic. Yet I wouldn't let him stop me from doing what I believed I should do. I played basketball. I wasn't a starter, but I got a lot of playing time as a sub on a team that made it to the state tournament. **If you want to win, you can't quit.**

✳ ✳ ✳ ✳

Flash forward 30 years. In July 1997, after 24 years with the General Electric Company in positions of increasing responsibility, I was made a corporate officer. I've already shared the story of Jack Welch and the silver money clip, and how special it was for a guy like me to reach the pinnacle of GE success. At this time, I held the title Vice President, Engineering Services for Industrial Control Systems, which had replaced the old GE Motors Division where I got my start. I led an organization of more than 1,800 personnel in the U.S., Canada, and Latin America—a challenge to say the least. The biggest challenge of all, however, was my boss, the CEO of Industrial Control Systems—a highly intelligent, hard-driving guy who believed in public ridicule as a management tool. Let's call him George.

At first, we got along well because I met and exceeded all performance expectations. On good terms with Jack Welch, George pushed him to make me an officer. He also pushed Jack to take it away.

In order to expand his business, George acquired three small companies that became my responsibility. No matter what I did, they did not deliver as expected. Some of this underperformance was my fault, and some of it reflected fundamental issues in the acquisitions themselves. I knew the GE creed: I was responsible for everything that happened under my watch. I expected to take the heat, but I didn't expect the full-on, personal, public assaults by my boss.

During regular operational reviews, he would berate me in front of my senior staff. "These results are totally unacceptable, Dobbs. In fact, these results are so bad, I don't know why you even bother coming to work. My daughter could do a better job than you. Your performance is shit, and you'll never make it." That's the way he treated me in front of MY staff. It was even worse when I had to meet with his senior staff.

My grandmother had died a few years earlier, and I thought of her a lot during this difficult time—thought of how she never gave up no matter how difficult the challenge. Finally, one Saturday, I went into George's office. He was listening to the stereo, and before acknowledging me he reached over to turn the volume up. "What do you want?" he asked.

"George," I said, "if you don't want me here, you're going to have to fire me, because you can't berate me enough to make me quit. I am not a quitter."

He looked at me like I was a pile of garbage that got dumped in the middle of the room. "Is that all you have to say?"

"That's it."

"Get out of my office."

I believe George told Jack Welch that I had asked to quit—which wasn't what I said at all, but I believe that's the way he played it. I was relieved of that job and lost my "stripes" as a GE officer just before my 25th anniversary with the company and one year after gaining the title for the first time. After 25 years, I prepared to leave GE and interviewed for other jobs. Then, over the July 4th weekend, I received a call from a guy named Jim Mohn, who had just taken over as CEO of a new acquisition called GE IT Solutions (ITS).

"Jack asked me to give you a call," he said. "I can offer you a position running our global service organization as executive vice president." This was not an officer position, but Jim assured me that Jack had promised to give me a shot to earn my stripes again if I delivered.

This was my biggest challenge yet, leading a field service team of some 5,500 technicians operating in North America, Latin America, Europe, and Australia. I initiated several key changes that raised revenue and profit margins in my sector, but the business as a whole was losing money, due to the challenges of integrating more than 40 smaller acquisitions into a single business unit. As business performance failed to improve, Jim Mohn ultimately left.

Following Jim's departure, the GE ITS business was broken into two divisions, one focusing on the North American market and the other on Europe. In April 2000, I asked to take over as CEO of the ITS North America business, and during an interview I received the position. At this time, the total ITS business had grown through acquisitions from $2 billion in annual revenue to $7 billion; yet the North American business was losing $100 million a year on a run-rate basis, the biggest money loser in the GE Company.

As I began my new position, Jack Welch laid out the ground rules loud and clear: "Randy, there isn't a single GE shareholder who's enamored with revenue. All they care about is earnings. We're not going to fix this with more growth. Those days are over. Do what you have to do to make this business profitable."

"Do I get my stripes back?" I asked.

"Absolutely." Not long after that, Jack invited me to another luncheon and presented me with another engraved silver money clip. "Randy," he said, "this one is special for me, and I know it's special for you, because you lost it and won it again." It was special, indeed, and I truly appreciated Jack's willingness to give me a second chance.

I ended up turning that GE ITS business around from losing $100 million a year to earning about $12 million. It was one of the most difficult assignments I've faced, and it was also one of my greatest successes. I'll share the story of how I accomplished that in a later chapter. For now, the most important point is this: I left GE after that assignment, after winning back my stripes as a corporate officer and earning the Turnaround Business of the Year Award. I left on *my* terms, as a winner. The reason I was able to leave on my terms? I absolutely refused to quit.

The biggest reward in not quitting is how you feel about yourself and about the next day you have to face. **If you want to win, you can't quit.**

CHAPTER 3

Ask for the Hard Jobs

I have often wondered if many 27-year-olds awake to a day away from their current job with as many butterflies and doubts as I awoke with on a cloudy morning in early 1977. I was staying in a hotel in Fort Wayne, Indiana, an old Midwestern town and site of GE Motors' headquarters. This morning—and the long, restless night before—reminded me of so many Friday nights when I had waited in a locker room, excited to be finally playing in a football game. Even though I had practiced hard all week, I still was so frightened of the unknown opponent and task in front of me, I had to force myself not to puke!

As I dressed in my best business suit, I asked myself over and over the same questions that had kept me up all night: "What am I doing here? Am I really good enough to play the position I am asking for in this big-time leadership league?" With knees knocking and stomach churning, I made my way to a job interview where my only real qualification consisted of a passion to do the job and a track record of good execution in lesser roles.

I'd heard a lot about Fort Wayne during my five years in the GE Motors business, but I'd never been here. The headquarters building proved much less impressive than what I had imagined back at the Jonesboro plant. When I reached my final destination, I found myself sitting in the very impressive office of Bill Fenoglio, the president of GE Motors. Somehow this small-town boy was on the top floor of the GE Motors headquarters, in an office filled with job mementos and other testimonies to business success, one after the other, waiting to talk to a guy who was more important than I could comprehend.

At that time, I had worked for five years in tough and risky positions at the GE Motors plant in Jonesboro. My career was moving quickly, even by GE standards; the plant manager in Jonesboro had taken me under his wing, personally assisting in my development and job opportunities. Now I was putting those five years of career growth on the line—interviewing for a job so far above my level of experience or qualifications, with such a high risk of failure, that the decision could only come from the leader at the top of the food chain.

Even more impressive than his office, Bill was a smart, charismatic guy in his early forties, definitely a few steps above anyone I had met at this point in my career...a guy I could see myself aspiring to be exactly like. In my short career, all I knew was the Jonesboro plant and the plant manager seemed like God. So standing before Bill Fenoglio felt like meeting God's God; yet I knew my next opportunity was to sell him rather than fear him.

As we discussed the position—formerly held by a longtime plant leader who had recently failed, then turned down by numerous better-qualified candidates—Bill leaned forward and asked me point blank: "Randy, tell me why a young guy with so much success in his first five years with GE would want a job that could end your career if you fail?"

The situation and my gut said, *This is no time to be a bullshitter, so tell it like it is.* "Mr. Fenoglio," I said, "I'm willing to take the risk because I believe that great risk will bring great reward. And if I fail by chance, I am young enough to start over." I wanted that job so much that I was worried, not about what I might do to lose, but what I could do to win.

I got the job.

✳ ✳ ✳ ✳

Anyone can do an easy job, and lots of people settle for the easy path in life and work. That's okay, if you don't have any real ambition, but if you want to distinguish yourself from the crowd—if you truly want to grow as a person and a leader—you have to ask for, take, and execute the hard jobs. You have to get out of your comfort zone, take calculated risks, and execute around those risks. Every troubled organization or business is waiting for a leader who will take risks, energize the employees, and *lead* them versus managing them. That's what I knew we needed when I interviewed with Bill Fenoglio.

I think of my grandmother, and her decision to leave her husband in California and return to Auburn as a single mom to care for her widowed mother and keep the family business running. She definitely asked for a hard job, a job that most women didn't ask for in the 1930s, and she dedicated herself to it for more than 25 years. She experienced plenty of tough times in those years, but she always took the hard job, the hard path, and executed for the good of the family.

When my grandmother's brother left to fight in World War II, she took over his general store next door to the laundry, while her father's former secretary ran the laundry. When her brother returned, too sick and injured to work in town, he retired to a country farm. The secretary saw this as a time of weakness for the Young family and an opportunity for herself. She left to start a competing laundry across town. Once again, my grandmother rose to the challenge, taking the hard job. She managed the laundry and the general store so successfully that she maintained and grew her customer base while warding off this new competition.

She believed anything was possible, and she had the willingness to tackle the hard jobs to prove it. Her moxie, her commitment, and her persistence in any job, hard or easy, gave me the strength to take that same approach in my career. Along with my refusal to quit, that willingness to take hard jobs stands as one of the top three elements of my success. It needs to become a big part of your own success. In fact, I don't think you can be a successful transformational leader without it.

I'd like to share a few specifics to give you an idea of how powerful taking the hard jobs—and having the successes and failure in those jobs—can be for your career.

I first worked at the GE motor plant in Jonesboro, Arkansas, as an hourly summer employee during college, laboring in a hot, smelly paint booth on the assembly line...not exactly a high profile entry to the GE world. My full-time career's inauspicious start was as a quality control specialist—a really great title for a quality-department gofer—at an annual salary of $10,000. It was the summer of 1973, and I had been out of college for a year, working as a sixth-grade teacher with a $6,000 salary. The GE salary offer floored me—my wife and I thought we were rich and didn't believe we could spend all that money!

In fact, I was the lowest-level salaried employee at the plant, and the Jonesboro plant was just a small bump on the global GE organization's broad face. Asking for hard jobs moved me up quickly in that plant, and hard, risky jobs kept my career opportunities and performance moving through the GE organization's multiple levels. In 1973, as a young man just out of an elementary-school classroom in Jonesboro, I could never have dreamed of achieving the levels that I ultimately achieved in the business world.

About two years into the job, a new line of small refrigerator motors was transferred to the plant. An IUE union plant, the facility had most employees on piecework, meaning they were paid per item produced, with daily goals set by time studies and governed by the union contract. Typically, union employees at our plant earned about 130% of base pay, working—in my opinion—not much more than seven of the eight hours of each shift. The plant manager decided this new product line would pay an hourly wage, eight hours pay for an eight-hour day, which triggered strong resistance from the employees. They saw it as a battle-ground for the whole plant changing. Output dropped substantially.

Faced with this difficult situation, management seemed uncertain and reluctant to lead. I saw the impasse as an opportunity and longed to get into the action of being a supervisor on the floor. So I volunteered to supervise that line during a difficult start-up period, in part because I thought I could do it, in part because I wanted more of a challenge, and in part because I was just plain bored with the quality-control job. One thing I have learned in my career: Hard jobs are never boring.

This first experience as a leader in the business world showed me I had a natural talent for it. I helped improve output somewhat by convincing the employees that it was in their best interest to serve criti-cal customers—because if we didn't serve our most critical customers, we'd lose jobs. I worked one-on-one with the employees and helped to resolve some minor issues, including convincing them to work more over-time. This kept up our production requirements, even if they were not willing to work as fast as management wanted. I was up front and honest, telling them that I could not resolve the biggest issue—their objection to piecework—but that didn't stop us from wanting to retain our customers and jobs.

This position only lasted about four months, but it had pushed the leadership button in me! I knew I could address adversity. I knew I could appeal to people via compassion, brutal honesty, hard work, and setting a good example. I knew I could only be happy in the business world when utilizing those skills. This product line ultimately went back to piecework, but we worked the overtime and focused on critical needs, helping us survive this difficult period.

In the year following that experience, I felt frustrated by my quality-control job and jumped aggressively at another leadership challenge in the same factory area as my first supervisory experience. That entire unit had fallen behind on output, and employee morale had plummeted. I asked to become the motor-assembly unit manager—a two-level promotion—and though there was resistance because of my inexperience, I got the job.

I called the supervisors together and discovered that they were just as frustrated as the production employees—which all came back to leadership, communication, and focus. They offered many good ideas to improve the situation. **For the first time in my career, I realized your job as a leader isn't to have all the answers.** It's to facilitate people to help you find the real answers. We put together a plan, implemented it, and worked diligently as a team to fix a real output and backlog problem. It took more than eight months, but that unit was on schedule, delivered our commitments to our customers, improved our backlog, and reduced our overall cost.

All I did was work with the people who knew the jobs best. I later forgot that lesson and had to relearn it in a more difficult situation. Yet once again, asking for a hard job took me to a whole new leadership level—leading other leaders.

As I managed my unit, another motor assembly line in a different unit developed serious quality issues. This was during the energy crisis, and GE had tried to make the motors more energy-efficient without improving their fundamental manufacturing processes or equipment. With my experience in quality control, I was certain we could fix the problem by understanding the machinery capabilities and retooling the machinery to get more accurate product specifications. It would be expensive and—most important and controversial—would require slowing down the production lines and our overall output during the retooling process.

I discussed this with the plant manager and asked for the opportunity to fix the problem as manager of quality control. This was the position that ultimately took me to Bill Fenoglio's office in Fort Wayne. When I told Bill I was willing to take the risk because I believed great risk would bring great reward, I meant every word of it. In truth, I wasn't worried so much about my own ability, confident I could figure out what was wrong. The real risk was whether I would receive support for the bold, unpopular actions I knew we would have to take.

On my first day as manager of quality control, our largest customer—GE Appliances—rejected 40,000 motors. Talk about a 27-year-old risk taker's rude welcome to the real world! The situation was even worse than I thought, and I quickly led my team to do increased quality inspections and process capability measurements on the production equipment.

As I suspected, the testing revealed centering problems on the machinery, exacerbated by the new energy-efficient design. I went to the plant manager and told him that we would have to shut down the line and retool. I suggested we do it in two phases, keeping one half running while retooling the other half.

The plant manager had been my mentor and sponsor ever since I began working at the plant. He saw I was willing to work long, hard hours and wouldn't take "no" for an answer. His support was critical to my getting the unit manager and quality control manager promotions. Not only did he mentor me, but he encouraged me to never accept "no" for an answer and make that an integral part of my leadership style.

Now I was telling him something he didn't want to hear, and this "no" caused our relationship to turn ugly. He wanted to improve quality, of course, but he was unwilling to make the necessary sacrifice of output during the time period required. So he tried to manage me with daily threats and screaming matches. I remember being in his office one day, and in a rage he screamed, "If I go down for lack of output, I'm going down with my hand around your throat!"

It just got worse, and I so feared disappointing the Fort Wayne leadership who had supported me in that job that I accepted a position with another motor company. Fort Wayne's upper management convinced me to stay with GE. In the end, we retooled the line in two phases over a six-month period, dramatically improving yield and outgoing quality. Yes, we suffered in output and even lost some market share—which we quickly regained once we retooled the lines, making our products the best on the market.

Shortly thereafter, the plant manager was fired. You can't manage successfully and win in hard jobs with fear and threats. You can't succeed if you're not willing to make tough decisions and take tough actions for the good of your customers and your company.

I remained at the GE plant and continued receiving promotions with even higher responsibility, ultimately becoming manager of shop operations, responsible for all production personnel across three shifts. The lesson was clear: Taking that hard job and standing up to my own boss, doing what I knew was right for the company, propelled me into the highest leadership levels at that plant. It taught me lessons that would stick with me forever.

These few examples from early in my career illustrate how taking the hard jobs became integral to my business approach throughout my life. After working 10 years in manufacturing at that one plant, it was a hard job to pack my family in the car and move to South Bend, Indiana, to begin a sales position that I was told would be good for my career. This time, my sponsor—the guy who told me I had to move into sales to learn more about the customer side of the business—was Bill Fenoglio.

Moving to South Bend with a young family in the middle of winter was tough, but it was even harder to tell my wife nine months later that we had to move to South Texas and learn the Mexican culture so that I could assume a position as plant manger in Reynosa, Mexico.

Much later, my single-hardest job was leaving GE, the only company I had ever worked for, and moving clear across the country to work for a Dutch company with a completely different organizational culture.

I'll share more details of these experiences in other chapters. For now, here's the key lesson to remember:

To truly succeed in the business world, to become an effective transformational leader, to learn about yourself through your successes and failures, you *have to take risks*. You have to put yourself in a position to really transform the business and transform yourself as a person. You have to get out of your comfort zone. You must **ask for, take, and execute the hard jobs.**

THE SECRET SAUCE

CHAPTER 4

Win Them Over...Communicate, Communicate, Communicate

In 1982, after spending less than a year in a new sales job in South Bend, Indiana—my first career and family move in GE—I was offered my dream job by GE Motors: plant manager! As I've shared with you, when I worked at the Jonesboro plant, I thought the plant manager was God, and I could never view myself as the God of a GE plant facility— though I dreamed of it all the time. Sometimes impossible business dreams come true because of location, timing, available candidates, or just plain luck! In this case it was a little of them all, but mostly the catch was location. The plant was in Reynosa, Mexico, just across the border from McAllen, Texas, where not a lot of up-and-coming leaders wanted to go. In fact, my wife said, "It's not the end of the world, but we can see it from here!"

The early 1980's marked the boom time for maquiladora projects, in which American companies utilize favorable Mexican laws to import raw materials and equipment into Mexico, employ less expensive Mexican workers to manufacture the products, and then re-import the products into the United States, all without duties or tariffs. The trade-off for Mexico was and still is the creation of solid jobs. In our plant, most workers were teenagers, which is a story in itself.

The Reynosa plant manufactured motors, primarily for central air conditioners. It was created to become the largest and most profitable of all GE motor plants, a sector where profits were really dwindling, by taking advantage of the maquiladora opportunity. I could share many great, funny stories about my Mexico experience, but for now here are two stories that demonstrate the importance of clear communication.

About one year after I arrived, a major fire occurred in a critical, one-of-a-kind production facility. To build electrical motors, we had to coat the copper windings with a liquid varnish and then heat them in an oven until the cured varnish insulated the windings. Every product in our plant had to pass through our single varnish treatment system. It caught fire one Tuesday morning just after the start of the 6:30 A.M. shift, with varnish burning and dripping from the roof into the plant facility.

My first story seems funny now but was drop-dead serious at the time. I was sitting at my desk in the main office building when I heard a weak knock on my open office door. I looked up to see Juan, my plant maintenance manager. "Please come in," I said in English. "You know my policy is always open door."

This concept of bringing the Big Boss—the Jefe General—a problem, or even being able to knock on God's door, was totally foreign to Mexican culture. Even my highest-ranking employees had not accepted the idea, and Juan was one of the plant's three highest-ranking Mexican employees. So he shuffled slowly into the office, too timid to make eye contact with me. "Buenos días, Juan," I said pleasantly. "How has the shift started?"

"Senior Randy," Juan replied. "We have a problem."

"Juan, you know I do not believe in shooting the messenger." (Messenger shooting is a big problem in Hispanic culture).

"Sí, Senior Randy, but the problem—she is a biiiiiig problem!"

"Juan no problem is so big that we can't face it together! So please tell me what it is."

"Senior Randy, the plant—she is on fire!!!!!!!!!!!!!"

My first communication lesson that morning: Leaders don't just talk about communications; they must force communications to happen for the good of their business. I would guess that Juan and I could have talked until I smelled smoke or saw fire from my office. You have to force *two-way* communications regardless of the issues, culture, timing, and/or perceptions. If the leader doesn't proactively drive communications, your business can be destroyed literally, emotionally, or financially from lack of knowledge!

We evacuated the plant in a panic, releasing hundreds of teenage workers into the street, where they made such a ruckus the Mexican authorities wanted to arrest me for disturbing the peace. I knew if I got arrested, the plant would probably burn down. So I asked my HR leader—the only Mexican-American on my senior staff—to "take one for the team" and be arrested as my proxy. He did, but the situation became more chaotic as our 500-gallon tank, where we stored water for just such an event, was about to run dry. Our ground water had such high salt content that we could not use it for firefighting purposes.

I asked one of the workers to climb atop the water tank and find out how much water we had left. "Como hacerlo?" he asked. *How do I do it?*

"Usa una ropa." I replied. *Use a rope.*

So he climbed the water tank with a rope in his hands. About ten minutes later, I left the fire-fighting activity, running back to the water tank, inquiring about the amount remaining. My biggest fear was that the tank would empty before the fire was put out. When I hollered up to the employee in Spanish, "How much water is in the tank?" he replied, "No se!" *I don't know.*

"What do you mean you don't know?" I yelled back in Spanish. "Just hold the rope up beside the tank so we can measure!"

"I cannot see the rope!" he yelled back in Spanish.

He had dropped the rope into the water and was trying to see the rope from the top of the tank floating in the water. He didn't understand—and I didn't communicate clearly—that he was to lower the rope until it touched the water, and maintain it at the water level so we could measure the remaining supply.

My second communications lesson that morning was this: Never assume everything you say is as clear to others as it is to you! Use visual aids; use others to deliver the message so more than one person understands; ask questions and/or do it many more times; but don't assume a clear image in your mind is at all clear to your employees.

Communication is hard work. Communication is critical to any venture's success. Communication stands as the rallying point or death threat to your business. It all depends on you to create clear, two-way communication.

Now the situation was desperate, and we really had to scramble. The local airport had a pumper truck but wanted about $200 in advance. The situation was in such disarray, I had no access to petty cash; so my senior staff and I emptied our pockets to come up with money, and the airport crew helped us put out the fire.

We saved the plant, but the fire set my new career and the plant operation back, and almost got me fired. More on that later, but for now, here is my point: Leaders communicate. Good leaders not only communicate clearly, but are aware of their audience, and adjust their communication for maximum effect.

Communication that exposes also establishes trust

First and foremost, if you want the single biggest key to effective transformational leadership, you have to *drive* the communication process. This builds trust and commitment among those you are tasked to lead. Building this trust will prove critical to all other future initiatives you drive to transform your organization. Without this hard-won trust, your organization simply will not commit to your leadership.

This complex process consists of many steps, but the first step is very simple: To transform people, you must share with them more about yourself than you may think you need to...who you are, where you came from, how you operate, and what you expect of them.

In all three companies I transformed as CEO, as well as in other high-level leadership positions earlier in my career, I began my initial meetings with all levels of employees by really opening up about myself. I am an extremely open and honest person by nature, and to me it's critical to establish this openness and honesty in my introductory presentation. With me, what you see is what you get—no hidden agendas, no games behind the scenes—and I believe this will win over many for the future journey. For those not won over, it will expedite their departure.

I am totally open about my past...how I grew up in a broken home, how I had to step between my abusive alcoholic stepfather and my mother and sisters, how I felt guilty leaving my sisters behind when I left home to save myself. I share the story of my college years, working full-time as a machinist, living on peanut-butter sandwiches, and getting by with four hours sleep a night. I tell them truthfully that I still keep my Class A Machinist's card because it allows me never to worry about having a job, which in turn lets them know I don't fear the challenges in front of me.

Many leaders would question sharing this kind of personal information. They feel they have to keep a "professional distance" to maintain a level of respect. Or they feel no need for "strangers" to know about their past.

I understand this kind of thinking—I really do—but it is flat-out wrong. All of us in the organization are just human beings. A CEO carries a good and bad history, just like any other employee. Therefore, I believe the more workers know about their leader, the more apt they are to trust and relate to their leader, and commit to following his or her leadership.

As for professional respect, well...if I can't earn your respect by being honest about who I really am, then I don't deserve your respect. Not every professional has respected my story, feeling it was too much about "Randy." Yet I have won more than I have lost, so I trust my way.

Most of my employees in every business have been pleasantly surprised and quickly engaged by my openness. I know this because I can see it in their eyes, their posture, and their nodding heads as I'm talking with them. Many employees also have told me in personal conversation or written communication how much they appreciated my candor. They have embraced me as a leader and my tough changes because they felt my ongoing and open communications were real, personal, and honest. I built genuine trust at all three companies I led and constantly worked to earn professional respect. That trust, commitment, and hard-earned respect is the foundation for all else to come in your challenging role as a transformational leader.

Among many stories about my introductory presentations at businesses I've led, the most pointed involves a fairly recent experience at USIS. When I arrived at USIS in February 2005, three separate businesses operated under the USIS umbrella. The largest by far, both in terms of revenue and number of employees, was the Investigative Services Division (ISD). This division provides a number of services to the federal government, the most important and financially lucrative being background investigations on federal employees, civilian and military, through which they obtain security clearances required to do their jobs. This valuable work became even more important following the terrorist attacks on September 11.

The heart and soul of the ISD business is a workforce of about

3,000 well-educated and highly trained field investigators who live and work in all 50 states as well as U.S. territories. These folks are an impressive group of professionals, extremely dedicated to our national security. They also are professional skeptics. A good investigator keeps probing for information until he or she is satisfied there's sufficient data to write a fair and comprehensive Report of Investigation. That report will either qualify or deny the subject a government security clearance.

I have faced a lot of tough audiences in my time, but the ISD investigators were the toughest, because they do not accept things at face value.

Making the situation even tougher, employee morale was very low when I arrived at USIS, and investigators' morale was as bad as in any of the divisions. Many of these highly trained, patriotic, and committed men and women were really questioning whether they should stay with the company; in fact, our annual turnover rate exceeded 20%! It costs more than $50,000 to properly train an investigator and takes six months of on-the-job experience for a new investigator to become productive. Losing even one good investigator is bad for the business and for national security.

Many reasons existed for this low morale and high turnover, and I will share further thoughts on employee morale in other chapters. For now, I'll just point out three key reasons for low investigator morale:

1) The previous leadership did little to drive communication. Adding to that problem was the high ratio of investigators to their immediate supervisor, the district manager (DM), which was on average 42 to 1! The former CEO, Phil Harper—in many ways an excellent leader—believed the best news was no news. This leadership style reflected his experience as a former Special Forces operative in Vietnam. Phil is very personable and charismatic, a great guy, but few employees ever got to meet him or hear from him personally. He was a face and voice in the quarterly newsletter, where he shared a brief, five-paragraph message four times a year.

Because Phil did not drive communication, most of the leaders working at USIS did not value communication. So it was not about lack of town halls or other communication. It was about a mindset, and this mindset went to supervisor-investigator ratios so large that **people lacked coaching, leadership interface, and a voice to anyone about**

their business frustrations. After five years of dramatic growth, many operating frustrations arose that I will address later.

2) The investigators were underpaid considering their level of education, training, and commitment. Most were college graduates, and the annual starting salary for an entry-level investigator was about $30,000. The structure allowed for very rigid advancement, with the ability to grow their annual salary to more than $50,000 as a senior investigator after four years; but not many achieved that senior investigator rank and tenure.

This advancement path was more time-based than performance-based, so many had no motivation to perform "above-and-beyond." Most of our investigators stuck with their job because they believed in the national-security mission, but they felt very bad about the pressure for performance with no voice for review. **Their chief frustration: recognition was time-based rather than performance-based.**

3) All the investigators were **made to feel that the numerous business issues**—including a 13-month backlog of work—**were their responsibility to own and fix, with little pay and no voice.**

My challenge when I arrived at USIS was to go out and convince 3,000 skeptical men and women that all this could and would get better; that they should give me a chance to turn the situation around before they decided whether to stay or leave the company. I quickly realized that USIS's future financial success almost completely centered on improving investigator turnover to less than 10%. How could I not begin with communication?

In my first 10 weeks at USIS, I conducted more than 20 town-hall meetings in as many different cities, speaking to almost 2,300 people... an exhausting but energizing experience. At each town hall, I started with a roomful of skeptics, many who sat in clearly wary poses, leaning back with arms crossed and heads tilted. They looked at me as if they were thinking, *Okay, I'll listen to what this new guy has to say, but if he's just our next guy in a suit who really doesn't care, I'm not buying it.*

As I began to speak, however, their postures and attitudes began to change. They uncrossed their arms and leaned forward in their chairs, really listening to my every word. They smiled and nodded their heads in agreement. At the end, they not only offered warm applause, but—more important—bombarded me with thoughtful, probing, and honest questions, giving me clear insight into where I needed to focus my energies. In fact, at every subsequent town hall after the first, I was able to open with what I had learned at the previous town halls. They received this even more warmly than my personal information, because it indicated I was listening and not denying the issues.

Next, you will find the PowerPoint presentation I used for all my introductory town halls at USIS, along with some comments on each slide. As you read through it, you will have a pretty good idea of what I discussed and how I presented it. Feel free to use this as a template for your own introductory presentation.

USIS ... ISD/PSD/CSD

Introduction
to
Randy Dobbs
(Plus Initial Thoughts/Impressions)

February 2005 – USIS Presentation – Randy Dobbs

At my third town hall meeting, when I projected this opening slide on the screen, I was asked if I was changing the company logo. I was taken by surprise, because I had created these charts before I came to USIS and had simply thrown a yellow, red, and blue block design in the upper left-hand corner to add a little color. Yet I was impressed by the question, because it clearly indicated the sensitivity of these employees to the USIS identity. It also indicated they were asking honest, off-the-cuff questions.

Although way too new to be changing the logo and colors, I would indeed alter them nine months later as part of an all-out effort to establish the USIS brand in a broader marketplace. I'll share that story later.

Some Background

- **Humble Beginnings**
  - **Broken Home/Tough Environment**

- **No "Silver Spoon"**
  - **Worked Way Through College**
  - **Real Life Experiences Formed Values**

- **Allegiances/Hard Work**
  - **25 Years One Company**
  - **15 Jobs Entry Level to Officer**

- **Team Builder/Real Person**
  - **High Energy/Strong Ethics/Lead by Example**

February 2005 – USIS Presentation – Randy Dobbs

The real takeaway on this slide was this: So many people came up to me or sent me emails after the town halls telling me how excited they were about my coming to the company. After hearing specific details of my life and work experience, they saw that I was a real person in the real world—and not many people would share these kinds of personal details. There are aspects of my story that almost anyone can relate to, and they were energized to know their new CEO was genuine just like they were.

What is Leadership?

- *Transforming* organizations to ensure long-term vitality
- *Doing the right thing* versus doing things right
- Driving an organization's attention through *vision*
- An effective leader is a *social architect*
- Accumulation of *trust*
- Deployment of self
    - persistence
    - willingness to take risks
    - commitment
    - consistency
- End result is *empowerment*

February 2005 – USIS Presentation – Randy Dobbs

This slide is all about setting expectations for the organization's leaders. The most gratifying aspect of this slide and its message was that many of the **good** district managers (and we had both good and bad) later told me in person or by email that this slide created a whole new set of expectations for them and their senior leaders, starting with me.

As I was writing this book, I also realized that this slide's first two words are "Transforming organizations," exactly what this book is about. This slide was created long before I began this book, and even longer before Paul Walker and I came up with the title and focus on transformational leadership.

Manager   vs.   Leader

• Depends on Title & Hierarchy	• Depends on Collaboration
• Presides over an Empire & New Ideas	• Thinks Cross-Functionally & Builds Informal Networks
• Controlling	• Delegating/Negotiating
• Rewards Bureaucracy	• Rewards Entrepreneurship
• Sets Standards & Rules	• Promotes Individual Initiative & Problem Solving
• "Carrot & Stick" Motivation	
• Rewards Based on Status	• Rewards Based on Contribution

New Employee Loyalty is Not to Manager or Company, but to the Opportunity for Personal Challenge and Growth

February 2005 – USIS Presentation – Randy Dobbs

The biggest laugh at every town hall came when I finished discussing this slide and said, "The good news for all of you is that, if you have one of these guys on the left, he's going to become one of the guys on the right or you won't see him anymore." That really got the investigators laughing—a combination of genuine humor and relief that USIS would no longer tolerate managers.

What You Can Expect From Me

- **Decisive Leadership ... Demanding, but Fair**

- **Lots of Energy ... Enthusiasm, Excitement, Energize the Team**

- **Frequent Communication ... Direct & Candid**

- **Timely Response**

- **Reward Performance ... Execution is the Key/Not Planning**

- **Team Player ... Very Supportive**

- **Willing to Take Risks ... But, Don't Like to Give or Get Surprises**

- **Credibility with me Comes from Meeting Your Commitments**

February 2005 – USIS Presentation – Randy Dobbs

This slide sets expectations **from** me and **for** me. More heads nodded "yes" to this slide than any other. They realized I wasn't just standing up there telling them what *they* had to do. I was telling them what I was going to do for them, and now I had to live up to it.

Personality Traits of RED

Positive Traits
- Demonstrates confidence that anything is possible if you want it bad enough
- Quick, decisive and confident in giving clear/direct leadership
- Obstacles are only those things you see when you take your eyes off the opportunities
- Judges others by their ability to think and act quickly
- Work culture is very simple: "Tell us what you are going to do, and do it"

Negative Traits
- Can be impatient at times, driven by will to win
- Can be very candid, almost blunt at times, to speed up process and understanding
- Can be bored with tasks that hold no interest for him

February 2005 – USIS Presentation – Randy Dobbs

This slide also got a lot of nods. They responded most to the fact that I presented negative traits. It takes guts to share what others have said bad about you, but it's very liberating, because you push those traits right out in front.

My Pet Peeves

- **Surprises ... problems can be dealt with, not surprises**

- **Less than full disclosure in communications**

- **Not doing what you said you would do**

- **Problems without proposed solutions**

- **Lack of allegiance to team**

February 2005 – USIS Presentation – Randy Dobbs

When I presented this slide, I said, "We're going to set the rules today. I'm the new CEO, and there aren't many things that are really pet peeves for me, but there are five big ones, and you've got a new set of rules."

When you read the five pet peeves, I think the takeaway is just what many employees said to me after the town halls: They perceived that I intended to be a fair, focused, and compassionate leader, but that I could not and would not tolerate anything but each individual employee taking responsibility for our business's success. I closed my discussion of this slide by saying, "I have two children who bring me enough surprises and problems without solutions, and I don't need seven thousand more." That always got a laugh, but it also got an important message across.

How Best to Interact With Me

- **Have Character** ... Integrity first & last, always do the right thing
- **Vision** ... Know where you are going, have a goal for every day
- **Planning** ... Assume nothing, expect things to go wrong, have a back-up plan and be flexible
- **Communications** ... Be brief & precise, make sure everyone understands your issues
- **Deliver** ... Results are expected, respond quickly if results are not being delivered
- **Change** ... Be prepared to move quickly following agreement
- **Team** ... WE WILL WIN OR LOSE AS A TEAM, NOT INDIVIDUALS

February 2005 – USIS Presentation – Randy Dobbs

This slide's key is the last bullet point. You can transform an organization as a team, but you can't transform it one individual at a time. I really emphasized that as I presented this slide—we were going to win or lose as a team.

CHAPTER 5

Vision to Reality...Never-ending Communication

The introductory town halls proved only the beginning of my USIS communication strategy. I drove regular, consistent corporate-wide communication though my personal efforts. My example led my senior leaders to drive communications in their organizations—which in turn led their leadership teams to drive communications on a local level. Within 18 months, the whole company went communication-crazy, and I mean "crazy" as a very positive term.

In the three years I served as USIS CEO, the company went from having one quarterly newsletter to a bi-weekly letter from the CEO, three divisional newsletters, regular HR newsletters...and I lost count of the local newsletters at the business unit, district, or department levels. Town halls became a staple, not just for me and my senior leaders, but for directors and managers throughout the business.

The heart and driving force behind this communication effort was the bi-weekly message I sent out as an email attachment to the whole organization. At the time I arrived at USIS, very few employees had email access, due to security concerns. So, while my team worked to provide more email access, we had the local manager post the message on a bulletin board and/or distribute photocopies by hand.

I sent my first bi-weekly message almost immediately after officially taking responsibility as CEO. That's when I met Paul Robert Walker, who co-wrote this book with me. He has become not only a valued business colleague, but also a good, trusted friend. Susan Rogers, our vice president for human resources, introduced me to Paul over the telephone. Susan told me that Paul had handled most USIS internal communications as a consultant since the company's early days. He had deep company knowledge and a career writing books for major publishers including National Geographic. That was enough for me. Paul and I hit it off over the phone, beginning a working relationship that continues to this day.

Like most high-level business leaders, I am a capable writer; but, also like most leaders, I have too much on my plate—too many decisions to make, too many meetings to attend, too many documents to read—to draft all of my messages myself. Every transformational leader can benefit from a professional writer and editor like Paul. At GE, we called writing professionals "speechwriters," and if you'd like some insight into that world, I recommend a wonderful, fun, and funny book called *Jacked Up*, written by Bill Lane, Jack Welch's primary speechwriter.

I am a natural public speaker, so I never needed a speechwriter. What I did need, however, was a partner in my communications strategy to transform USIS *one message at a time*. We called this bi-weekly message, "AskRandy," though Paul joked it should have been called "Randy Speaks." On one level, he was right, because this became my platform to talk to each and every employee, just as I had spoken to our town-hall audiences. However, as I emphasized in Chapter 4, effective communication is always two-way, and we also used the AskRandy program to drive communication from the employees.

Later in this chapter, I will share three AskRandy messages from three different time periods, so you can get an idea of how I communicated and how the communication changed as the company culture changed. First, however, I'd like to share with you the transformational power of totally opening yourself to the complaints, concerns, and creative ideas of the people you lead.

I had originally envisioned that employees would write to me at my regular business address: **randy.dobbs@usis.com**. I had created a similar regular message program at both GE and Philips, and the employees at both organizations knew I had an open door in the physical world and an open mailbox in the virtual world. Those excellent two-way communication programs yielded powerful results. However, the USIS AskRandy program proved the most sophisticated two-way program I have ever created. This was due to two factors: 1) It was my third try, and I used everything I had learned from the first two programs; and 2) I had a partner who brought talent, commitment, and company knowledge to the partnership. Although Paul was a consultant rather than an employee, he embraced the AskRandy program as if it were his own and was never hesitant to remind me of messaging needed for the USIS audience.

Before we released the first AskRandy message, Paul called me and said, "Randy, I just realized that if we are going to send out this message entitled 'AskRandy,' we should have an AskRandy mailbox where employees can direct their questions and concerns." I immediately knew it was a great idea and asked him to set up the mailbox before we released. That is another key trait of a transformational leader: when you receive a good idea, say "Yes" and run with it.

Paul set up the mailbox so he could monitor it for me. Then we sent out a preliminary email to all employees, announcing that this mailbox was now open for their input, and I would be following with my first bi-weekly message the next day. We got five responses to this preliminary message, but that only hinted at the avalanche to come.

In the first two months, we received about 200 AskRandy emails from employees! These smart, dedicated, and creative people were so desperate for someone to listen to their concerns, they flooded cyber-space (or at least my cyberspace). Paul organized the emails for me, and created a document every two weeks containing the latest batch of emails, presented chronologically. If Paul had specific knowledge of the issue or the person who wrote the email, he would add his comments, which I found very helpful. Remember, this flood of emails came to me in my first two months on the job. I was just learning about the company, and those first 200 emails were an eye-opening experience!

I printed out the documents Paul sent me and read them whenever I could, writing my thoughts and responses in the margin. Then, on the weekend, I sat with my laptop at home and **answered every single email personally—all 200!** I knew that if I answered enough emails personally, the message would get out that I was really listening; that I was absolutely serious about considering employee concerns as one of the driving forces in transforming USIS. Most of these messages were not good news, but if you really want to drive open communication you must learn to live with that fact. Leaders must not only have a thick skin but must also understand the importance of interpreting and acting on bad news.

I knew this could not go on much longer. After two months I had developed a clear vision of my first steps to begin the USIS transformation. I could no longer spend so much time answering every single employee's concerns. I still valued those concerns and was dedicated to resolving them appropriately, but I had a responsibility to move on to macro-level initiatives. So we began Phase 2 of the AskRandy program.

By that time, I had changed all but one of my senior leaders, and I'll discuss that transition in Chapter 7. I felt I was hiring the best people for the business. I knew I could only drive true change by putting people on my staff who valued communication as I do. So I decided it was time to turn the AskRandy program over to my senior staff.

Paul continued to monitor the incoming emails, but now, instead of preparing a document for me, he forwarded them to the appropriate senior leader. For example, if an employee from the Investigative Services Division voiced a concern related to daily operations, Paul would forward the email to the divisional president. If the concern or suggestion dealt with an IT issue, he would forward it to our IT leader and copy the divisional president. I no longer saw these emails, though my senior staff often brought to my attention ideas or concerns that came out of AskRandy emails.

My main concern at this point was that every email be answered, and I made it clear to my senior staff that this was a serious responsibility. We asked these senior leaders to copy the AskRandy email address with their response, so Paul could track and save them. If he did not see a response within a week, Paul sent a polite reminder to the senior leader. As a long-time consultant rather than an employee, Paul had no qualms about giving my senior staff a firm push when necessary, because a) they couldn't fire him; and b) he knew I stood solidly behind him.

Over time, the flood of emails became a steady flow, then ultimately a trickle, down to three or four emails a week. To some extent, this diminishing flow was due to the fact that almost everyone with a burning issue, concern, or idea had already gotten it off his or her chest. However, the more important reason was our creating many other vehicles for two-way communication. My senior leaders drove communication in their own organizations through newsletters, telecons, town halls, etc. They made it clear that, like me, they had an open-door policy and that open door included their USIS email addresses. This openness on the senior level inspired a new openness on the local level. After having no one to listen to their concerns before I arrived, USIS employees now found eager ears at every level.

Phase 3 of the AskRandy program began about 10 months after I arrived, when I hired a highly experienced and talented director of communications named Michael John. Michael came with a truly impressive communications background. He had spent 20-plus years in the Navy and rose to the rank of Captain, working in communications and public relations. His assignments included speech writing and communications counsel for several high-level elected government officials, members of Congress, key cabinet members in two administrations, and about a dozen admirals who led major Navy commands. He also had extensive experience as a communications executive in the public sector.

It took Michael a few months to get the lay of the land, just as it took me a few months. During this period, Paul continued to write the AskRandy messages with me, and monitored the AskRandy mailbox, while Michael became more and more involved in working with me on the messaging. Finally, Michael took over the AskRandy program completely, collaborating with me on the messages and making sure my senior staff addressed the employee concerns expressed in the AskRandy emails. By this time, Paul had plenty of writing and editorial work producing our divisional newsletters.

During this third phase, the frequency of the AskRandy messages changed from every two weeks to every month or so, as the situation required. We had so many other communication vehicles that I no longer needed to carry the ball.

As the CEO it was my responsibility to establish a culture of two-way communication, and that is exactly what I did. We distributed a total of 53 AskRandy messages between my introductory message on March 17, 2005 and my final one on July 23, 2008. That's when I announced I was stepping down as CEO and introduced the incoming CEO to the entire USIS team. Those messages provide a comprehensive history of a dynamic company during a period of transformation. To give you a sense of my approach to these communications, I am including the first section of three very different AskRandy messages below: the introductory message and two others from key times in my effort to transform the company. (If you would like to read the complete text of these messages, you can find them in the Appendix, pp. 164-171.)

Everyone has an individual voice, of course, but perhaps these three messages will stimulate your thoughts about your own voice, and the importance of communication from a transformational leader.

Below you'll see my first AskRandy message, sent out March 17, 2005, just 2½ weeks after joining USIS. By that time, I had already led several town halls. I wanted the employees to know the town halls were only the beginning, and that I would communicate with them on a regular basis. I also wanted them to know that, although I was driving the communication process on the front end, real communication could only begin when they responded and communicated to me. I always kept the employee-audience in mind in everything I did and communicated. This first message contained some of the same data I had shared at the town hall meetings. Although I had met with almost 2,300 employees, that represented only a third of USIS's 7,000-member workforce.

This first AskRandy elicited 22 responses and opened the gates for the flood that followed.

TO: All USIS Employees

FROM: Randy Dobbs

AskRandy   Number 1   March 18, 2005

It is with great pleasure and enthusiasm that I join USIS as CEO at this exciting time in the company's development. Though I have only been part of the USIS community for fifteen days now, I appreciate the warm welcome I have received and am impressed by the high level of demonstrated commitment to our success. You are all responsible for this success, but I want to offer a special thanks to Phil Harper and his executive team. Their pioneering efforts have established a solid groundwork for the dynamic growth opportunities ahead.

As we move forward together, I will report to all USIS employees every other Friday in a letter addressing our successes, opportunities, and challenges. I ask that each and every one of you reference these messages in your daily work and strategic planning. By doing this, we will collectively continue to build momentum that will enable us to mature and develop our position as a premier supplier of security services.

I call these letters "AskRandy," because I want you to know that I am here to answer important questions you may have about our company, its present, and its future. I encourage you to contact me with these questions by email at AskRandy@usis.com. Since not everyone has access to email at this time, we are in the process of setting up a voicemail number. For now, let's begin with what is probably uppermost in your mind: Who am I, why was I selected for this position, and what does my selection mean to you and the USIS team?

You can read the full text of this AskRandy in the Appendix, pp. 164-165.

Next is AskRandy #24, sent out on March 3, 2006, the week of my one-year anniversary as CEO—which equates to a business-wide electronic message to all employees every two weeks. I think it's a helpful sample to share, because it captures both what we had accomplished in that year and what we had to focus on the next year.

You will notice that the overall look of this AskRandy message substantially differs from the first message. In that first year I worked with my senior leaders to change the company logo, colors, tagline, vision statement, and other aspects of the USIS brand. This was a major step in moving away from being viewed primarily as a federal government-support business to being viewed as an international security business with strong service offerings in both the governmental and commercial worlds. I will share some of the thinking behind this rebranding in a later chapter.

TO: All USIS Employees

FROM: Randy Dobbs

As I write this message, my excitement continues to grow regarding the future of USIS. This week marks my one-year anniversary as your CEO, an appropriate time to look toward the future while considering the past. Even more exciting to me, however, are the first-ever USIS strategic planning sessions that we held in the Minneapolis-St. Paul area last week. In this AskRandy message, I'd like to share my thoughts on this first year and these first strategy sessions.

When I reflect on the journey we've taken together during the last year, I continue to be pleased by all we've accomplished. I have discussed many of those accomplishments in previous messages, but I would like to share with you what I consider to be the three most important total-business accomplishments: 1) we have strengthened leadership throughout the organization; 2) we are on a firmer financial footing, which will facilitate future growth; and 3) we are establishing a stronger, clearer, and more comprehensive USIS identity in the marketplace.

It's satisfying to take a moment to celebrate a milestone like this, but I am also very aware that the completion of one year means the beginning of another. I look forward with enthusiasm and optimism to the challenges and opportunities that lie ahead. We still have more to do, but we have a great team that will take us where we need to go. The strategic planning sessions gave me an opportunity to see our top leaders and their direct reports focused not only on performance but on great ideas to strategically grow the company in the future. I was very impressed by the quality of our leadership teams.

You can read the full text of this AskRandy in the Appendix, pp. 166–167.

Below is AskRandy #41, sent out on March 30, 2007—as I began my third year with USIS. By this time, I had communicated so much and so frequently with our employees that I felt they were ready for an in-depth analysis of the state of the business. This would have been unthinkable when I first arrived. At that time, the frontline employees did not understand how the state of the business affected their daily lives. During the first two years, through the AskRandy program, I had given them a course in Business 101—and now they understood that only successful, growing businesses can reward their employees the way they want to be rewarded.

By this time, the look of the AskRandy messages had changed further. We put this out during Phase 3 of the AskRandy program, when Michael John, who recently had been promoted to vice president for corporate communication and creative services (CCCS), had taken over Paul's role. As leader of the Creative Services group, Michael worked with our graphic designers to come up with a logo and more professional look for the AskRandy communications. It is also interesting to note that Michael rather than Paul worked on this message with me, and the most careful reader would be hard pressed to find any difference in the voice. This is what talented communications professionals like Michael and Paul do: They work with the leader's voice and suggest ideas and refinements without interjecting their own voices. You, as a transformational leader, must take responsibility for establishing and maintaining your own voice. Though you will need to work with communications professionals, you have to ensure that the final product represents your tone and leadership direction.

You can read the full text of this AskRandy in the Appendix, pp. 168-171.

Finally, I would like to share an email sent out under my name on Veteran's Day of 2005, my first year with USIS. This email demonstrates why it is so important to work with a communications professional who really understands your vision and the company culture, and "owns" the communication process as if it were his. At the time we sent this email, we had just finished our first-ever Leadership Conference, bringing 300 of our top leaders together for three days in Orlando, Florida. The conference was a big success, and we continued them as long as I served as CEO. However, it also required an incredible amount of energy and focus from me and many others in the organization.

After the conference, I planned to head home to Atlanta for a well-deserved long weekend—my first break since joining USIS more than eight months earlier. Paul and I put out a regular AskRandy message on Thursday, November 10, and I flew to Atlanta that evening. The next morning, Paul checked the AskRandy mailbox and found an employee email saying that he was disappointed that the AskRandy had not mentioned Veterans' Day. He pointed out rightly that many USIS employees were veterans and that some employees were currently on active duty in Afghanistan and Iraq.

Paul immediately realized we had made a faux pas by not honoring the many USIS veterans. He wrote the brief email below, and, in my absence, reached out to Bill Mixon, the president of our largest division, ISD, and a veteran himself. As Paul later told me the story, he reached Bill on a golf course, just as he was about to chip up to the green (Bill was taking his first day off). They talked, and Bill told him the email was a great idea. With that green light, Paul ran with it, and tracked down our "corporate spammer" in the Information Technology group—one of the few people who had the technical permissions necessary to send an email to the whole organization.

The email went out around 3 P.M. Eastern time, and we immediately began receiving emails from employees expressing their pleasure and pride in the message. We hit a home run with this, and it became a tradition every Memorial Day and Veterans' Day to honor the brave men and women who served our country in the military. None of this would have happened if I had not had a communications professional like Paul and a business leader like Bill who knew the right thing to do and felt empowered to do it.

Here's the email—just 54 words, but those words really resonated with our employees.

On this Veterans' Day, I would like to acknowledge all our veterans
and thank them for their service. We owe you a debt of gratitude
for your dedication, bravery, and self-sacrifice. You have made this
a better world, and we as a company are dedicated to preserving
and strengthening the security you have forged.

Randy

In the Appendix, p. 172, you can find the 2007 Veterans' Day message to see how we continued to develop this theme.

Listen and probe

Throughout this chapter and Chapter 4, I have emphasized the importance of two-way communication. However, even the most open and honest two-way communication will not reveal all the information a leader needs to transform an organization or business. A transformational leader must **listen** very carefully to what his employees say, and then **probe** for further information. This is not just an exercise in empathy, but the best path to new insights and ideas for your business's performance. Let me give you a general example before I get into some specifics.

Let's say an employee tells you he's unhappy with his job. That's unfortunate for both the employee and the company, but it doesn't tell you anything specific on which you can take action. You have to probe to discover the reasons why the employee is unhappy. It may take a lot of careful listening and probing before you understand the factors, but that is only the beginning. Now you must probe further, not with the unhappy employee, but with various leaders throughout the business. Together you must determine if the concerns are valid and—most important—how the concerns might be best addressed, and if addressing them will help the business as well as the employee.

I have already shared with you that many USIS investigators were unhappy with their jobs when I arrived and the three key factors causing their unhappiness: 1) poor communication at the senior and local levels, exacerbated by the high ratio of investigators to district managers; 2) relatively low pay with a long road to advancement, based on time rather than merit; 3) expecting the investigators to own every operational problem without giving them a voice to express their concerns and ideas.

Once I fully understood these factors, I knew they were fixable and that fixing them was essential to USIS's business success. In the following chapters, I will share with you some of the details of how we fixed them, as well as how I solved problems at GE and Philips.

In the first couple of months at each company, I introduced myself, drove never-ending communications, and began to formulate the vision. However, you can't fully formulate or accomplish the vision until you establish ownership among the leaders—and ultimately the employees—of issues facing the business. The next chapter is about engaging your senior leaders to help further define the vision and the necessary steps to turn the vision into reality.

CHAPTER 6

Send Them to the Marriott

No, I am not writing this chapter for compensation or recognition from a major hotel chain for using their name. If you will bear with me, I hope to share with you how critical this title and action are to the transformational process.

First, let me tell you how rewarding and cruel the world of big business can be to those who really care and strive to do their best. In 2002, I won the GE Turnaround Business of the Year award. Jeff Immelt had recently succeeded Jack Welch as CEO, so in some respects the award tasted even sweeter to me, because Jeff had initiated this award and made the final choice for its recipient.

Whenever a new CEO takes over a company, every employee wonders what will change and how the change will affect him or her. This was no different for me. Although I was CEO of a GE Capital business, Jeff was still the big boss, and I was two steps removed in the GE hierarchy. I reported to Mike Neal, who, as President and Chief Operating Officer of GE Capital Corporation, reported into the GE Corporate structure. So to me, this award not only affirmed my current business success but also seemed like a sign that I'd receive further opportunities under Jeff's leadership, just as I had under Jack's. It turned out that assumption could not have been further from the truth.

Although my turnaround at GE IT Services was the pinnacle of my GE business career to that point, in many ways it was a terrible job, involving many days when I dreaded going to work. As mentioned in the introduction, I eliminated almost half of the workforce. Changing people's lives in this way always causes me to lose sleep. As is normally the case, we also dramatically attacked non-payroll costs. It's no walk in the park to tell the survivors they will receive even less resources to do a tough job with little chance of getting better any time soon.

I will share some of these stories in more detail later in the book, but my main point for now is that I performed a very tough job well and deserved to move into a leadership role in a growth business; but that is not how the new CEO viewed me fitting into his new world of challenges. I was one of Jack's guys, not Jeff's, and—just as important—I was 52 years old now. It was clear to me that Jeff wanted to develop a younger leadership team.

Although I respected Jeff, I got the word from my new boss, Art Harper, VP for GE Capital, that Jeff saw me as a "fixer" and strong operating guy–not a guy he would move into a growth role in a growth business. To some extent, I feel Jeff was right. I was a strong "turnaround" leader who could size up a business's issues, rally the organization, and drive change to improve the performance. I more than proved this at ITS. However, what really threw me was Jeff's message through Art was that as long as ITS existed, and as long as I performed, they were happy to have me there. However, it was clear that Jeff had no intention of using me in any other role, something hard to believe and accept after two grueling years of fixing the worst business in all of GE!

I believed I'd be a GE guy forever—I joked that the GE logo was branded on my ass—but after 27-plus years and becoming an officer twice, I decided not to give up on myself and my capabilities, but to discover if I could perform outside my lifelong employment setting. I was angry, confused, disappointed in the way I was being treated, and saw no chance of getting the kind of assignment within GE that I felt I deserved based on my performance. So it was my responsibility to drive this change!

My job search produced three appealing opportunities: CEO of a publicly traded software company in Huntsville, Alabama; chief operating officer (COO) of a tool manufacturing company in the Northeast; and CEO of Philips Medical Systems, North America, which required moving to Seattle, Washington.

On a personal level, the Alabama position was most appealing, because of my roots and because my family was located in Atlanta. However, in terms of my career, I chose Philips, based on a previous assignment in GE Medical Systems, my diagnostic imaging market knowledge, and the business integration success experienced at ITS.

Also, I had spent my entire career with GE, one of the largest companies in the world, and Philips, a very large corporation based in the Netherlands but with operations around the world, appreciated and needed the GE corporate cultural best practices...and I could bring those to them. The Philips position offered a return to a business that I loved and gave me a sense of satisfaction: selling and servicing medical products that made a positive difference in the world.

Sequestering the Philips leaders

Philips had recently made a major bet in the medical business industry by purchasing four unique medical equipment and service companies for around $5 billion. Following these acquisitions, they had relocated their North American headquarters from Connecticut to Seattle. So I was stepping into a very new situation where I could make a difference in so many ways as a change agent, an integration leader, a growth guru, and a cost zealot. They offered great products and services, but their leadership structure languished in disarray due to the many overlapping functions following the acquisitions; and the planned revenue/earnings performance fell significantly off the mark. I had faced a similar, tough situation at IT Solutions and felt I knew how to successfully address it.

On the day I officially reported to work as the new CEO, most of my senior leaders were in Hawaii for an annual recognition event for high performers. This particular event, to my surprise, had unusually large attendance and stretched out over several weeks to include high performers from all of Philips's new acquisitions.

First impressions and pace of change start with the leaders and especially with those who report directly to you. I felt concerned that, while Philips had recently acquired four other businesses and was missing its financial objectives, a large group of leaders with less than committed thinking were spending weeks versus days in Hawaii. So my first day on the job involved flying to Hawaii, meeting the senior leaders, understanding their views on the business issues, introducing Randy Dobbs (with similar slides to those in Chapter 4), and determining which leaders would help me transform Philips Medical Systems.

From day one, I began the process of deciding who would leave this business, but it felt very different from my removals to just survive at GE IT Systems. In a growth business, you don't have to remove the front-line employees; you need them and want to develop them. Removing ineffective leaders is a different matter. On a professional level, a leader who doesn't lead, who doesn't improve all other employees' future opportunities, doesn't deserve to be a leader. However, on a personal level, removing any employees—including senior leaders—changing their lives and significant financial resources in most instances, is never easy and shouldn't be if you are a true transformational leader.

I flew to Hawaii from Atlanta direct—a LONG flight. I arrived about midday and that afternoon began to meet and interview several senior leaders. It's important to share with you the five critical actions/questions I used in this exploratory interview process beyond the introductory slides to Randy Dobbs:

1) I listened a lot and took copious notes!

2) I asked all my senior leaders for direct-report "A-player" names (top performers) and then spent 30 minutes interviewing each A-player within 30 days.

3) I asked all senior leaders and A-players to tell me about themselves from their first job out of school to their present assignment, which will tell you much about their communications capability.

4) I listened and looked for three key attributes: intellect, passion, and track record.

5) I asked a final and key question: "If you had my job starting today, what are the top three things you would do?"

I interviewed more of my senior leaders the next morning and played golf that same afternoon with three *second-tier* leaders. I wanted to make a statement to the senior leaders that I was just as interested in getting to know the second tier, and I felt I could use the golf course setting to gain strong insight into issues from the second-tier perspective. It also would get the word out that this Dobbs guy is a real person who cares and is focused on driving change at all levels.

This is an essential lesson for every CEO. Senior leaders may or may not survive the changes you bring to the business. If they are not valuable to the company's future direction, you as a transformational leader want to know who is moving up the ladder behind them. That second-tier leader also may or may not survive the changes, but in that second tier you can often find important future leaders who will become critical to both the business's future and your transformation. The same lesson applies to leaders at any level: You have to get to know and understand the leaders and employees who report to your direct reports.

After two and a half days at the Hawaii event, I left my senior team with many thoughts and perhaps a few fears. I flew back to Seattle, where I spent my first night in a new town. The next morning, I reported to a new building where more than 1,200 employees—who did not go to Hawaii—were waiting to see who I was and what I was going to bring to their business. I believe my first victory with the headquarters team was that I did not remain in Hawaii, but flew back in mid-week to meet with them. My first day in Seattle, I focused on a series of employee town halls similar to those for USIS that I described in Chapter 4.

The receptivity from the majority of the people, as in most of my other assignments, proved positive. They quickly opened up to me because they believed I was a real person with a real commitment to making their work life better. I quickly sensed in these initial meetings that they really cared for this Philips Medical Systems business and that they wanted to make a difference. This is true with most jobs where people willingly go and spend the majority of their waking hours. However, their frustration was clearly visible. Many felt we were under-performing and that the leadership was far removed from the needs and issues that could improve the business.

In this lies another critical element of transformational leadership: In every business, the employees who really know the company's issues and the potential solutions are at the working level. It is your job as the transformational leader to identify the processes for obtaining this information and prioritize them into a list of items to implement and execute. Since you can't interview thousands of employees, let me reveal a critical part of the secret sauce: It identifies, prioritizes and implements the solutions to transform your business, regardless of its condition.

As mentioned before, I listened at the organization's many levels and took lots of notes. At the end of each day, I consolidated the issues into buckets of problems including operations, communications, purchasing, quality, organization, structure, information technology, compensation…the bucket list goes on and on the more you reach out and listen. I then compared the buckets of issues to the top three issues that my senior leaders and their direct reports had given me. I drew critical conclusions from all this data and formalized the top 10 to 15 issues for the business.

Now I needed ownership of these issues and the proposed solutions at a level where the resources existed and the work could get done. That work of identifying solutions and implementing them did not fall on me—which would have been the surest route to failure for me in my leadership role at a new company.

At my first staff meeting some six weeks into the job, I reviewed with my senior staff much of the consolidated bucket-list information I had gathered and the conclusions I had drawn about the business's most critical issues. While that list may not surprise you, let me give you my top five conclusions:

1) No real integration of the five companies despite integration teams with more than 12 months of work behind them;

2) No one company brand...many of the various locations still displayed their previous company signs, carried previous company business cards, and celebrated previous company events, even after 12 months;

3) Information technology integration had no ownership for one-company issues, and financial reporting consisted of a spreadsheet consolidation at the end of the month;

4) Sales teams still called on customers representing their respective products, and multiple regional structures in the businesses did not integrate;

5) North American relationships with the product factories were abysmal, and the customer was less important than finding fault internally.

I don't have to tell you the other top five to 10 issues. Things were much worse than I was told during the interview process. (I bet that has never happened to any of you before!) So, at this Friday staff meeting, after I had reviewed the conclusions and issues with the senior team— whom I had now known for all of six weeks—I asked them to tell me by Monday who would replace them for an undetermined period of time for day-to-day business needs. This request left many with dropped jaws. I made it because I had a reservation and a conference room for them starting the next Tuesday at the local Marriott. On Monday I got the names of their replacements, and on Tuesday they began the process of identifying the solutions, the resources needed to implement those solutions, and the implementation timeline.

I made myself available every day for consultation, and it was mandatory that they reported one day a week on their progress or issues that they needed help in resolving. At first, they did not like the process, and it took awhile to get real ownership. However, when they understood their working future hung on the line and embraced the process as not optional, they helped me lead the business down a two-year path of fixes/changes that resulted in significant financial improvement, market-share gain, lower turnover, improved cash flow, and substantial growth in sales. I also quickly discerned who was with me on this journey and who would have to go, both at my senior leadership level and among their direct reports.

As you will see in more detail in the same process at USIS, a key aspect of the sequestering experience is that the business runs day-to-day without the current senior team. You get to know the next level and the day-to-day business process much quicker while the senior team works on the transformational changes that will improve future performance.

Last but not least, the senior staff figures out quickly that they either will become a part of the solution or have no role in the new business. I lost senior leaders at Philips, some through the Marriott process and some after we formed the solutions.

After six weeks at the Marriott, the business had prioritized its needs and issues, agreed on the actions to resolve them, and the communications and actions had begun to drive change. At this point, communication becomes even more critical to a highly dispersed organization. Everyone (all 5,000 employees in this case) needs to know the business solutions and that the priority "train" has left the station. Their choice now, in whatever role they play in these business changes, is "get on the train" or "get left at the station!"

In the Appendix, pp. 185-189, I have attached some significant documents that illustrate how we as a team, via this process, had embraced the issues by late April 2003 and created both a game plan for the fix and a detailed implementation plan. All of this work led to a great results report-out to the Philips Board of Management (BoM) in November 2004, which is also in the Appendix, pp. 189-191.

To the Marriott at USIS

The Philips Marriott experience was so successful that I decided to take the same approach at USIS. As I've shared with you, my first two months at USIS included some 20 town-hall meetings in 20 different locations. Although I did meet with employees of our other divisions—the Professional Services Division (PSD) and Commercial Services Division (CSD)—most of these town halls focused on the Investigative Services Division (ISD), by far the largest division in terms of employees and revenue. In fact, ISD accounted for about 60% of USIS's revenue and 80% of earnings. That was the good news. The bad news was that ISD earnings had not grown proportionately with its revenue, and—as I have shared—employee morale was low, so low that we had a 20% turnover among investigators.

The #1 priority in the total USIS business was to improve earnings or grow EBITDA (Earnings before Interest, Taxes, Depreciation, and Amortization). My quick assessment of how best to do that was to lessen investigator turnover to around 10%, lower our training and hiring costs, and improve output from a more than 10-month backlog of work. This huge pile of cash was just waiting for attention. Numerous subsets of critical issues surrounded turnover and output, but they were not fixable without improving our investigators' desire to stay and work hard to achieve these goals. So I decided to limit the sequestering experience to ISD leaders.

The ISD president had an impressive military record, but did not practice the leadership style I embraced. Although every individual is different, many old-school military officers tend to utilize a command-and-control, top-down leadership style. While this may work in some places, I believe the best business leadership style is bottom up, where employees are empowered to voice their concerns and not only suggest but own the solutions. The president was planning to retire soon, and I accelerated that retirement. First I sent him and his senior leaders to the Marriott in Cranberry, Pennsylvania, not far from what was then the USIS headquarters in an old iron mine in Boyers, Pennsylvania—where we were co-located with our largest customer, the federal government's Field Office of Personnel Management (OPM).

The core of the ISD senior staff included a hard-working young woman named Michelle Rubie-Smith, who served as vice president for field operations; six business unit directors (BUDs...essentially field regional managers); the program manager of our largest non-OPM contract; and Jim Shope, the VP for Western Pennsylvania (WPA) operations. The WPA workforce included a variety of roles supporting the field investigators, ranging from data-entry workers to high-level reviewers who reviewed the Reports of Investigation and made necessary corrections and additions before sending them on to OPM.

I also requested that two other leaders join the meetings: ISD Director of Finance and Accounting Mike Santelli and ISD Director of Human Resources Susan Parent, both young dynamic leaders who turned out to be shining stars on the Marriott team. Although Mike and Susan reported to the senior leader in their functional areas rather than the divisional president, they played an integral day-to-day role in the ISD business. The Marriott process always must have a facilitator. I chose Dave Logan, a bright guy who, like Mike Santelli, was in the second tier of the finance and accounting department, reporting to USIS CFO Phil Sweeney—the one real keeper on the senior leadership team I inherited. Phil became a critical partner who represented the past but supported me unconditionally as I looked for resources like Mike and Dave to drive the future.

I sent this entire group to the Marriott in mid-March, just a month or so after I joined the company. I asked them to commit to staying there for two weeks and told them that I expected a full report-out detailing their ideas for addressing the issues in the ISD business and proposing the necessary solutions.

To get them started, I shared what I had gathered as the critical issues from my town halls, the inputs I had received during various interviews, and the three critical questions I was asking at all levels of the organization. I was very clear on the lack of OPM relationship, lack of investigator empowerment, organizational structure needs, and numerous technical issues, including lack of centralized records, excessive paper processes, no electronic timesheets, no email/Outlook access for investigators, and transcribing handwritten case papers. I asked them to consider three critical "questions of interest":

1) How do we grow the business and maintain and increase overall efficiencies? Simply put, what actions are necessary for productivity...more output at less cost?

2) How do we use technology as an enabler for change?

3) How do we continue to reduce the backlog in investigative cases while lowering costs, enabling us to improve both customer relations and earnings?

Troubled businesses typically house many competent people frustrated by poor leadership and organization. I soon felt I had discovered a number of those jewels, and I was letting them shine. I received some great, detailed, and well-considered answers to these questions, but I also received too many responses that had not been completely thought through. This exercise alone educated me in further understanding the ISD business, and it also helped me to identify talent for this business's demanding future.

The three questions of interest were just the beginning, and the team worked though many other exercises during the two-week period. The four additional business topics that ultimately produced broad creative solutions were: 1) How do you think the business and the team are doing relative to our market and our customers? 2) What are the top three to five priorities for this business to succeed? 3) How will this business's revenue, earnings, processes, and productivity be better next year? 4) If this were your business, what would you do differently?

They remained sequestered at the Marriott from a Monday morning, through the weekend, until the next Friday. While they were working together, I was still conducting town halls, listening to front-line employees, and interviewing additional leaders playing significant roles in the business units and other departments. This continued my "listen and probe" strategy, like building a house from the ground up.

While the ISD leaders were teaming at the Marriott, I continued to grow my insights about the business and calculate what solutions offered the best odds of success. I had no "magic solution" for all of the issues, but I was pretty clear on the problems and was actively forming potential solutions. I have always considered the first 100 days to be the most critical to my transformational success via my visibility, learning, and—most important—actions coming from that first 100 days. In the Appendix, pp. 173-177, you'll find my initial 100-day plan developed before I officially began at USIS and my expanded 100-day plan developed as my knowledge grew 30 days into the job.

On the second Friday, I came to the Marriott and the leaders gave their reports. By this time, I had added an old friend to the team, John Moore, as vice president of operations. John and I had collaborated on several occasions at GE, including the Mexico experience. In many companies the VP of operations runs the day-to-day company performance, similar to a chief operating officer (COO). John had a very different assignment: to analyze our operations and look for cost efficiencies and better ways of doing things. One of my most trusted business colleagues and a good friend, John made a huge impact on people, productivity, and performance. So it was great to have him with me as we started down the ISD business's change journey.

The first report-out proved less than satisfactory for two basic reasons: First, the changes were not hard-hitting enough, which I believe resulted from lack of previous empowerment to find and own solutions. Second, I believe they felt I knew the answers, and they did not want to conflict with my opinion. I had to deal with both issues or ISD was doomed to mediocrity.

By this time, our leaders had been away from their personal lives for 12 days, so I told them to go home for the weekend and be back Monday morning for another session. The second session ended up lasting three weeks, so these leaders were sequestered for a total of five weeks—a significant commitment by all.

The fact that I continued to gather information from all the organization's levels, including their direct reports—and that the business continued in its normal rhythm without them—made them more than a little nervous. As I mentioned earlier in this chapter, it's important that your leaders understand they are not indispensable. That was a key aspect of the sequestering process at both Philips and USIS—to find out which leaders brought value and which did not, and for them all to learn that the business can and did run without them!

The next report-out—a significant improvement over the first— took place in a hotel near our new headquarters in Falls Church, Virginia. I gained great insight into the problems we faced and the road we had to follow to solve them. One of the most valuable ideas from this session drove significant business improvement on all fronts: to create a team-leader position as an accessible coach, mentor, and span-breaker between the district manager (DM) and the investigators. This would address the problem of the high ratio of investigators reporting to the DM while also freeing the DM to take full ownership and drive the financial results of his or her district.

For the final chapter of this leadership exercise, I requested the business unit directors to return to their offices on Monday morning, after five weeks of absence, and spend a week with their respective teams. They would follow up with a report-out to me the following week on the reactions and plans to implement the changes. Although the WPA support staff was absolutely critical to our success, the heart of revenue production was in the business units. I had to understand exactly what was transpiring in each unit, and whether the director possessed the business vision and leadership strength to implement changes we needed to succeed. Also, privately, I had asked the ISD president to step down after the first report-out, as it was clear he would limit creativity and change. His exit freed his former direct reports to think and act much more creatively.

To conclude this chapter, I asked Paul to interview the three survivors of the Marriott experience. These three leaders really drove the process, and have significantly grown their careers at USIS. Not surprisingly, Mike Santelli and Susan Parent are two of the three. Mike recently became president of a new USIS division, Information Management, while Susan is now vice president of human resources for the USIS business. The third leader, Robert Calamia, was then director of the Central Business Unit (CBU) and is now vice president of ISD field operations.

All three of these leaders are sharp and committed, and they have some interesting insights to share about their experience back in the spring of 2005. As the guy who conceived this experience, I was both intrigued and gratified reading their written thoughts. Although I talked to all three of them many times while I was CEO, this was the first time I heard many of these thoughts and stories. Enjoy!

Mike Santelli

"At first I thought the whole exercise was irresponsible and excessive. I was a finance guy, I knew the numbers, and ISD wasn't crashing and burning. We were making our numbers, and pulling all the leaders out for such a long period of time seemed a little on the dramatic side. At the same time, I knew in my core that there were problems in the business and that we had to look for ways to change. My boss, Phil Sweeney, was CFO of the whole company, so we had a little broader view than some of the ISD operations people. I knew that this was going to be a big wake-up call. There were three things I took away from this:

"One, there was a new sheriff in town, and the guy had done this before. I knew this wasn't Randy's first time around the block with this tactic. He was going to get results, and if we weren't the team to do it, he would bring in another team. We quickly found out who was capable of getting it done and who wasn't—it was kind of like when you turn on the light in the kitchen at night and the roaches scatter. You could see people scurrying to cover their ass, versus being constructive and figuring out how we're going to rebuild this thing. There's nowhere to hide when that kind of pressure is on you.

"Another big takeaway was, I remember thinking how can we possibly be away from our day jobs for two weeks? And what the experience taught us is that we had some really good people underneath us. We can sometimes act as shade trees for the people below us, and by removing the shade trees for two weeks the sun can shine on the next level of leadership. It forced us to think about succession plans and boosted the people below us who were ready to step up—they ran the store while we were away.

"I also quickly saw that a lot of people were so wound up on the deliverables and picking at the numbers in detail that they wanted to make the report-out a master's thesis. I guess I'm more in tune with Randy's leadership approach, and I was pretty sure from the beginning that what Randy wanted was creative thought, new ways of doing things, and people who leaned forward, got that we had to change, and at least took a stab in a short period of time at alternative scenarios without perfect information.

"I was in on the finance exercises, obviously, and I remember people asking me, 'Are you sure those numbers are right?' I said, 'Look guys, Randy doesn't care right now whether the overhead rate is 30% or 35%. He just wants to see new ideas based on reasonable numbers, even if the numbers aren't fully baked.' The fact that I have an MBA helped me with some of the exercises, because they were not that different from the case studies we did in business school."

Susan Parent

"My clearest memory of the experience is that on the last day, after five weeks of being sequestered, I was so exhausted and numb that I slammed my car trunk on my hand, and it took me 30 seconds before I even realized it hurt!

"Another strong memory is that I later developed an appreciation for the facilitator, Dave Logan, that I did not have at the time of the Marriott experience. Since Randy wasn't there, Dave represented the force that was keeping us in this confining and bizarre situation. He reported to Randy by phone every evening, telling him how the sessions had gone that day, and we always had someone outside his door, eavesdropping and trying to hear everything he was saying. That bit of subterfuge was indicative of our basic problem during the first two-week session: we thought Randy knew the answers and that we were supposed to come up with the answers he knew. That's why our first report-out was not accepted. After that rejection, we began thinking more creatively and found some real answers to the problems we faced.

"As you'd expect with any group of strong individuals stuck together for five weeks, there was a lot of fighting, but there was also a lot of bonding and team-building."

Robert Calamia

"I was excited when I heard that we had a new CEO, because I believed we needed change. But the Marriot experience began for me with a high level of anxiety. I received a call from my boss, Michelle Rubie-Smith, telling me that I was supposed to be at the Cranberry

Marriott next Monday for a two-week session to discuss changes in the ISD business and that I had to pick someone to do my job while I was away. I was okay with that, but then I received a call from Judy Thompson, who was acting as Randy's executive assistant, telling me that Randy would be visiting the CBU the following week and wanted me to suggest two districts to visit for a town hall and interviews with leaders. I suggested Chicago and Oklahoma City, my two strongest districts with the strongest leadership.

"So I walked into the Marriott that Monday morning knowing that, while I was locked away in this hotel for two weeks, Randy would be visiting my business unit, hearing from investigators, and talking with my staff and the staffs of my district offices. All the other BUDs at the Marriott faced the same experience. To us it felt like a long, slow execution.

"At that time, I was married with two babies, one and two years old, as well as two older step-children. It was tough to leave that burden on my wife, but she understood that I was fighting for my job. I told her I was probably going to be fired, and she said, 'Things happen, and we'll get through it together.' I'm fortunate to have a woman like that behind me.

"Despite that fear, I thought the exercises and the sequestering were a good idea. As a business unit director (BUD), I knew many of the problems facing the business and was happy that we had a new leader who was working to fix them. I wanted to be part of the solution rather than part of the problem.

"My fears escalated when, at the end of the second report-out, Randy ordered the BUDs to go back to our business units and return to Falls Church in one week with a full report on the state of the unit. There was a rumor flying around that Randy didn't like PowerPoint—which wasn't true at all—but I figured, *How the heck am I going to do this report without PowerPoint?* So I went back to Chicago and worked hard with my district managers and business unit operations manager (BUOM), Cassandra Atkinson. Cassandra has left the company to pursue other opportunities, but she was an outstanding asset for me, first as a district manager (DM) and then as BUOM.

"Cassandra and I put together about 80 slides, and she accompanied me to Falls Church to give our report. When we arrived in the conference room, there was a single person there—Ed Hahn, who had been an outstanding DM for me in the Oklahoma City District and had recently been promoted to director of the Southern Business Unit. Ed had a hangdog look on his face and told me that he had just been removed from the BUD position. I consider Ed a friend, and he is still with the company today in a high-level business analyst position. On that day, however, the fact that a friend and trusted colleague had just been canned didn't boost my confidence.

"Ed left, and Randy came into the room and sat down right next to me. Randy is a pleasant looking guy on a day-to-day basis, but at that moment he had his game face on, and it was a scary sight to see. He stared at me, boring through me with those pale blue eyes. Bill Mixon had just begun as ISD president that day. He came in a few minutes later and sat down on the other side of me. I'm a big guy, and there I was sandwiched between the two big bosses with Cassandra on the other side of the room.

"Cassandra and I went though our presentation for the next three hours. When it was over Randy stood up and said, 'Robert, I have visited all of the business units, and you are the only BUD who no one had a bad thing to say about. Your presentation was top-notch." Then he reached out, shook my hand, and said, 'Thanks for doing a great job.'

"Honestly, that was the highlight of my business career to that point. Not only did I receive confirmation from the CEO that my job was safe, but I also felt a personal connection to a leader whom I knew was different than any leader I had met before. At that time I was 36 years old, on my way up the corporate ladder, but I lacked confidence. The fact that I was so afraid to lose my job and came out golden shows that lack. That day, Randy gave me a new level of confidence.

"As you can guess, I'm a Randy Dobbs fan, and I'm also a fan of Bill Mixon, who is now my CEO. Bill and Randy are different people, but they have similar leadership styles, and their style works for me. I hope to run my own business some day, and if I do, I'll pattern my leadership approach after Randy and Bill."

✳ ✳ ✳ ✳

Paul told me that Mike, Susan, and Robert all clearly remembered and spoke at length about an incident that occurred during the second report-out. We were having serious problems with our largest non-OPM customer, and I had recently received an excellent letter from the DM of a Los Angeles district dedicated to that contract, detailing the problems as she saw them on the ground, most of which emanated from the project management office located in our Falls Church headquarters.

I read this letter aloud to the group, and the project manager stood up and tried to defend himself, saying the letter was a bunch of BS and blaming everyone except himself. It was obvious to me that this guy was incapable of doing his job or improving the situation, and I decided to make an example of him. I came down on him pretty hard in front of the group; as Mike Santelli told Paul, "It was brutal to watch."

This was out of character for me. I do not believe in public ridicule, having experienced it myself at GE, and I usually do my dressing downs alone with the individual behind closed doors. But this was an unusual situation, with a group that had been together for five weeks, and the guy's excuses were pitiful. One thing I can't stand in the business world is a leader who can't lead and blames everyone else when he should be looking in the mirror.

Beyond the content of the report-out, one of the big things I learned from this five-week period of intense work was which leaders I could count on. During the time they were sequestered, I had hired Bill Mixon, who had worked for me at Philips, to lead the leaders, a key addition to my senior staff. I now had John Moore and Bill with me, one from GE, the other from Philips, and I continued to build my senior staff in the following weeks. That was the next step. Now that we knew where we had to go, for ISD at least, I had to hire leaders who could make the vision a reality, not just for ISD but for the whole USIS organization.

CHAPTER 7

Bring In Senior Leaders Who Can Get It Done

Transforming a business or any other organization is like preparing a great meal: If you don't have all the right ingredients, you will be very disappointed with the outcome. Your senior leadership team is an essential ingredient to get the Secret Sauce right. You have to find the right people—either inside or outside the business—with the right skills to drive the changes needed to transform the business. What matters is using the best ingredients or people.

I like sports analogies, so let me share a few.

If a baseball team had all the right players in every position, they would win the World Series every year. However, in reality, even teams with very high payrolls are almost always missing something. They may have an awesome batting order but insufficient pitching. Or they may have great pitching but too few guys who can get on base and drive in runs.

My old hometown team, the Atlanta Braves, is a perfect example of the latter. From 1991 to 2005, the Braves were one of the most dominant teams in baseball. They won their division championship 14 consecutive times and went to the World Series five times in the '90s. Yet they only won the Series once, in 1995. Why? During the mid-'90s, they had one of the strongest pitching staffs ever assembled, anchored by three future Hall of Famers: Greg Maddux, John Smoltz, and Tom Glavine. They touted some good hitters, too, but just didn't have the right guy in every position; so they came up short again and again.

To look at this another way, think of great individual stars whose legacies would lack their luster if not for the commitment to excellence by those supporting them. Unable to walk without braces from the age of 11 because of a series of childhood illnesses, Wilma Rudolph sprinted to victory in the 100-meter and 200-meter dashes in the 1960 Summer Olympics. However, her greatest thrill was capturing an unprecedented third gold medal on the record-setting 400-meter relay team, her skills surrounded by the right other three runners.

After being cut by the Pittsburgh Steelers and relegated to playing for a Pittsburgh semi-pro team in 1955, quarterback Johnny Unitas went on to star with the Baltimore Colts. He completed 26 of 40 passes to lead a no-name but dedicated Baltimore team to a 23-17 overtime victory over the New York Giants in the 1958 NFL championship game.

These were two unique and talented people who reached the pinnacle of success because they were surrounded by the right people.

That's how it is in the business world, if you really want to be a transformational leader and set new business records. No matter how smart and talented you are as a leader, you'll never transform the business until you surround yourself with the right team. Not only do you have to assemble the right team, you have to empower your staff to do what needs to be done, and they must cascade empowerment throughout the organization, believing they too can succeed as transformational leaders.

During my years at GE, I saw the best and the worst of this in my own leaders. I wish I could have learned this lesson earlier in my career by working for this type of leader, as I later did with an inspirational and empowering leader named Jim DelMauro at GE Medical Systems. More about Jim later, but first I'd like to share one of my toughest learning experiences about the importance of empowerment.

I learned the hard way in my first transformative GE job, serving as plant manager at the maquiladora operation in Reynosa, Mexico. I've already shared some details about this operation and the disastrous fire we faced early in my tenure. The fire set us back, but we had other problems, too, including language and cultural issues. However, looking back, I was the biggest transformational hindrance. I was so excited about this chance to be the big man, so full of confidence and energy, that I inserted myself into every decision without really listening to the very good team already in place.

When I arrived, the plant was producing about 20,000 motors per week, and my initial assignment was to increase output to 50,000 motors. The workforce was mostly kids, 16-18 years old, and the turn-over was 90-100% a year, which meant we were constantly training new workers. I had a senior staff of seven Anglos and one Mexican-American, who led the human resources function.

Following the fire, we got the factory running again within a week, but the operating situation remained dire, which increased my desire to take complete control. During these trying days, I received a phone call from my boss and former Jonesboro plant manager Bob Etien, inform-ing me that headquarters felt I might have been promoted too quickly. They were coming for a visit to assess the issues and my plans for recov-ery. While it wasn't said directly, the message was clear: I was failing! It was the first time in my career that I had faced truly significant failure, and it was a humbling experience.

I called my staff together for breakfast and explained the situation. Fortunately, one guy—John Moore, who was manager of plant opera-tions—had the courage to speak up. He told me flat out that we could fix the problems if I allowed everyone to do their jobs and stopped trying to do everything myself. I had been too naïve to realize that success is not about how much you control, but how much you let go.

As I mentioned in Chapter 6, John is one of my closest friends today. Over the course of the 20-plus years since the Reynosa experi-ence, he has worked for me in two other critical positions at two other companies. When I first took over the Reynosa plant, however, John and I got off to a rocky start. He had worked at the plant for a couple of years and had interviewed twice for the plant manager job. He lost the first opportunity to my predecessor, then lost the second opportu-nity to me. John is a smart and talented guy who had worked in Mexico for years, was fluent in the language, and understood the culture. I can fully understand today, and had some understanding then, of why John would resent this new guy who suddenly arrived to run the operation. In time, I won John over as an ally, and he became my right-hand man as we tackled the Reynosa plant's problems.

Working together as a team, my staff and I created a plan to improve production. When the top executives came to visit, we presented the plan and asked for 60 days to implement it. They gave us that time, and we totally turned the situation around, raising production to 50,000 motors per week and later 100,000, making it the most productive and profitable plant in the GE Motors Division.

I will share more details about how we accomplished this in a later chapter, but for now I want to emphasize the idea of building a senior leadership team. That doesn't just mean building a team for a particular situation in a single job—although a good leader must do that. This is something much bigger. Throughout your career, you must look for talented allies, building a cadre of leaders whom you trust and who trust you. John Moore was my first big "find," and I've asked John to share some thoughts about our first experience working together.

John Moore

"Randy was just a pup when I first met him. He was 34, confident and more than a little cocky, and I was 42. As Randy points out, I'd worked in Mexico for years, and I was definitely disappointed that I had lost out on the plant manager job for the second time—even more difficult for me because I had lost to this young guy who, as far as I knew, had never even been on the Mexican side of the border. When he first arrived, I wasn't inclined to go out of my way to help him; looking back I think that, despite our age difference, it was I who was being immature.

"It didn't take long for Randy to win me over. There wasn't any one epiphany; it was just watching him work hard every day, being consistent in his approach, trying his best to solve every problem we faced. I thought, 'This guy's really trying.' So I decided to help him in any way I could, and that was the beginning of a friendship and mutually beneficial working relationship that has continued on and off for more than 20 years. I also realized that I better get my head turned around or I was going to be out of a job. Randy was on fire, and I didn't want to be on the wrong end of that blowtorch.

"To understand how I looked at Randy in those days, I have to share a story from a GE maquiladora meeting in Mexico City. The main speaker at one session was Jack Welch's top VP for human resources, and at the end of his speech someone asked him, 'How do you get ahead?' At first, I thought it was a pretty dumb question, but when I heard the answer I changed my mind.

"The VP said, 'You've got to have a friend who can help you, and if you don't have one, you have to get a friend who can help you. How do you get a friend? You earn that friendship.'

"As I got to know Randy better and saw the way he approached leadership on a daily basis, I perceived that he was a guy who was going places, and that he could be the friend I needed to help me get ahead. I was right, but first I had to earn that friendship. Once I got my head on straight, I busted my butt in every way I could. Sometime after the meeting when I told him to let us do our jobs, he asked me to run the senior staff meetings we had every morning, so he could focus on larger business issues. In effect, I was running the plant on a daily basis, and I pushed the envelope as far as I could. You know you're doing a good job when your boss tells you that you've gone too far this time. That's how Randy and I worked together. I pushed production and other aspects until he told me I had to tone it down a notch. It's like becoming foxhole buddies. We've definitely been through the business wars together.

"Randy did turn out to be that friend, and he helped me to win my first GE plant manager job in Juarez, Mexico, just across the Rio Grade from El Paso. I was still working for Randy in Reynosa, and I know he was sorry to see me go, but he knew what I wanted, and it was his letter of recommendation that landed the job for me. He's given me a couple of other great opportunities over the years, but I'll let him share those as he tells his story."

❋ ❋ ❋ ❋

John is a great friend, but, more important, he is an example of the kind of leader I have looked for in every leadership job I have held. Over the years, I have developed a clear list of what I am and am not looking for in leaders who join my transformational team. I'm not looking for someone who wants a big title. I'm not looking for the smartest guy or gal in the world. And I'm certainly not looking for someone with all the answers. Here's what I *am* looking for:

1) People who can **see the changes** I am outlining to them as I gain understanding and insight into the business, and see driving those changes **as an opportunity for the business, for their own financial success, and for their career development.**

2) People with a **strong belief in themselves** and **confidence that my vision of the future isn't the only vision** for overcoming challenges we face. **People who bring something to the party.**

3) People who want to **build an organization in which they are**

respected. I don't want them to do it because they are anointed or because Randy said so. I want **people who build a dynamic, successful organization because they have earned the respect of their team.**

Looking at the list of these three attributes I want in my senior leaders, I realize that these are three of my strongest attributes. As a transformational leader, it's only natural to look for other leaders who share your best attributes.

However, I am not looking for someone who is just like me. In fact, diversity of experience and point of view make a transformational team even stronger. What I am looking for—and what you should look for as a transformational leader—are people who share my core values in the way they approach the business. Sometimes I become close friends with these leaders, as I did with John Moore. Sometimes our personal relationship is more formal, and that's fine. All that matters is that they possess those three attributes I outlined above. As long as a leader exercises those, then I know he or she can help me transform any business.

I received six more assignments at GE after the Reynosa experience, including a final position as CEO of GE Capital, IT Solutions, before moving on to the CEO positions at Philips and USIS. Each move was a step forward in my career, and as I worked through the challenges of each position, I continued to build a cadre of senior leaders in whom I could place complete trust. To go back to sports analogies, it's like putting together a Dream Team. I still haven't filled every position on my Dream Team, but I've filled a few of them with really great leaders. I will introduce you to two more in this chapter and also share some experiences I had with leaders who didn't make the cut.

My most significant promotional opportunity came in 1990, when I left GE Motors after 17 years and crossed GE business lines to GE Medical Systems as general manager for service in the Southeastern region of the U.S., where the newly promoted GE VP of Services, Jim DelMauro, was given the task of building a completely new North American service team. GE had decided they were going to change the game in the medical business. Instead of selling expensive equipment and underpricing services, we were going to sell service contracts to our existing and new customer base, placing more emphasis on performance and reliability versus new technology features.

After the down-and-dirty, price-sensitive world of factory operations, moving to GE Medical Systems was like Cinderella moving into Prince Charming's castle. The significant margin performance made us much less focused on cost and expenses as long as we were growing the business. That was not the world I had lived in at GE Motors. I worked hard to be open to this world, but I also took the opportunity to drive new thinking about cost and be that transformational leader that Jim DelMauro had taken a risk on, placing me in his largest, most profitable North American region.

I led an 800-employee service organization operating in 10 states. I had to call on everything I had learned about leadership up to that time to command a "virtual organization" I couldn't see or touch on a personal basis. I communicated regularly by telephone and email, but it was paramount that I travel extensively to meet and maintain relationships with as many team members as possible. Later, I would establish significant metrics and operating parameters, but I knew that communicating and touching the team and customers would be the heart of my job.

Our headquarters was on the outskirts of Atlanta, a major improvement over McAllen, Texas. This was my longest single assignment at GE—six years—a period of stability for my family and of my own personal and professional growth. Living in Atlanta, I also was able to spend time with my grandmother, who had returned to Auburn to live out her final years.

It was at GE Medical Systems that I met a talented HR leader named Karen Query. My service organization was closely aligned to the sales organization for the same geographic region, and Karen interviewed for a dual position as HR manager supporting both organizations. So she had to pass muster with my counterpart in sales as well as with me, and she came through with flying colors. Karen had been with GE for more than 10 years at that point, so she brought a strong understanding of the GE culture.

Karen proved to be a great ally in meeting the HR challenges of leading a large, dispersed organization. We became such in-synch working partners that I helped place her at two other GE positions, ultimately retaining her as a consultant—after she left GE—at Philips and USIS for HR best-practice leadership. I've asked Karen to share her insights into our business relationship and our shared approach to human resources.

Karen Query

"I first met Randy when I interviewed for the dual HR manager position at GE Medical Systems in the Atlanta area. As I went through the interview process, he laid out to me in true Randy fashion exactly what he was looking for in an HR leader, what some of the challenges were facing the organization, and how he wanted to steer the human resources function. What really struck me in this first interview was that Randy viewed HR as a strategic partner in the organization, helping to drive change and growth alongside operations and other functional areas. As I worked with Randy, I discovered that, while a lot of people say they want to use HR in this way, Randy actually does it. I learned as much from Randy being his HR manager as I did from any HR manager to whom I reported.

"As Randy mentions above, I followed him as an employee two different times at GE, and then as a consultant at Philips and USIS. So he has been very instrumental in helping me become the HR manager and the person I am today.

"This is another theme in Randy's career, and I've been fortunate to observe a lot of it. He is very good at people-intensive businesses, because he has great people skills and is an excellent communicator. He's able to develop a story, explain that story in a very understandable way, and help people see that story as a vision and what it's going to mean to an individual employee in terms of his or her individual success and the success of the business. That is one of his greatest strengths as a leader—to communicate the vision and obtain buy-in throughout the organization.

"From a human resources perspective, if you understand his methodology, his style of leadership, and his general approach to the business, you can quickly support the kind of HR strategy that it takes to be successful. That includes things like leadership development, leadership selection, team management, team support, and providing the training and initiatives that people need to be empowered. Randy strongly feels that it's important for people to have individual ownership of the business, and the ability to make individual decisions that they feel are important for the business.

"In preparing for this interview I made a list of the qualities that Randy looks for as he puts together his staff. I know he offered his own list earlier in the chapter, but these are some things I've seen while working beside him as his HR leader during hiring processes. He looks for leaders with 1) results orientation, 2) communication skills, 3) teamwork, 4) empowerment, 5) integrity, 6) change orientation, and 7) energy.

"Randy is very methodical in everything he does, and when he hires a senior leader, he creates a matrix of the qualities he is looking for and evaluates each candidate in all the qualities in that matrix. As an HR leader, I believe it's a great approach, and it has produced some great leaders. Randy is also a phenomenal coach, and if he sees potential in someone lower in the organization, or if he sees one of his senior leaders struggling but still believes in that person, he will invest the time and energy to help that individual become the best leader he or she can be.

"In closing, let me say that Randy has high expectations of himself, and he has high expectations of his leaders. Once you prove that you can meet those expectations, he is very loyal and that loyalty inspires loyalty in others—one reason why I've worked with him in five different jobs."

✳ ✳ ✳ ✳

I have had many experiences placing and removing leaders. The single-most dramatic experience occurred when I broke away from GE after 25 years, and took the assignment as CEO of Philips Medical Systems, North America. As I mentioned earlier, this job actually started at a recognition event in Hawaii, and on my second afternoon I played golf with a group of second-tier leaders. I did this consciously because, as I shared in the Marriott story, it's important for your senior leaders to know they are not indispensible and that a whole group of leaders works behind them, whom I will always reach out to so I can learn more about the business and validate what I'm hearing at the senior level. Also, it's essential to assess the talent, skills, and desire to succeed at the next level.

As the new CEO, I was expected to speak at the awards banquet and help recognize performance—a difficult task, because I knew no one. However, I did take this opportunity to introduce myself and communicate my PowerPoint slides...yes, even in Hawaii, where business was the last thing on people's minds, I began to sell the Randy Dobbs approach, very similar to what I shared in Chapter 4. So very quickly the supposed top performers knew who the new guy was and, more important, what was coming when they got back home. My message was also delivered during meals, group gatherings, and one-on-one meetings. The message was simple: I'm the new CEO. I'm happy to be here. We're going to take these acquired companies and establish one team. We're going to create a culture of openness, performance, accountability, and market leadership. I hope that as a high-value performer, you can achieve in this one-team environment and be with us at the celebration next year.

A young guy named Bill Mixon, then leader of sales operations, helped with the logistics of this awards banquet. A second-tier leader, he reported to the VP of sales who reported to me. Every job is important, but Bill's job was especially important for a second-tier leader. Sales would drive company growth, and Bill led and understood all of the back-office functions that supported the sales staff. I soon came to understand that Bill's insights and capabilities were much stronger than I realized when we first met in Hawaii. At that time, I just saw a bright, confident, energetic young guy who knew what needed to be done and had a tremendous desire to be promoted!

I asked Bill Mixon to join the senior leaders at the Marriott, the only second-tier leader I asked to do that. I included Bill because of the key role he played in sales and because of his previous business-integration work. He was a seasoned Philips leader, with a clear view of the organization integration issue. I had also discovered that Bill had strong communication skills and knew he would be an asset during the Marriott experience. I believed Bill possessed the courage of conviction for change.

While my senior leaders were sequestered at the Marriott, I continued gathering information through interviews with other leaders and local town hall meetings. Then, after receiving the report-out from my senior leaders, I embarked on a series of business reviews and town halls throughout the country. Bill accompanied me on many of these trips. Although I did most of the talking and fielded most of the questions, Bill offered his insights into sales and other aspects of the operational side.

After two months of information gathering, I determined the biggest problem facing Philips Medical Systems: too many chiefs and not enough warriors. The five separate companies had accomplished little integration. We still supported too many leaders, not just at the senior level but at the next two levels. Many responsibilities overlapped among the leaders, typical any time one business acquires another. The problem was especially acute at Philips, because the original business had acquired not one, but four other companies.

I decided we needed to remove approximately 250 leadership roles and titles...a dramatic move, but my information gathering had made it clear that it was the right thing to do for Philips' future. This extended the time at the Marriott. I tasked the senior leaders with achieving a consolidated organization within their own functional areas and giving me a targeted number of positions to accomplish this.

One of the leaders I personally removed was the vice president of customer service, a critically important position. We were a service business, and if you don't have top-notch service in a service business, you don't have anything. You can't keep your existing customers, and it doesn't matter how many new customers your sales team captures, because you won't keep them long, either.

To fill this key service position, I brought in a guy I had known at GE, who did a great job of establishing the processes and organizational competence we needed. However, he never adjusted to the Philips culture. So about a year after he arrived, I had to part ways with an old friend and business associate. Our friendship ended with his leaving, and, while I still regret that very much, I did what I had to do to maintain my leadership values and style.

I believe in second chances, and even third chances. As Karen Query mentioned, my talent for coaching other leaders is one of my favorite aspects of being a CEO. My love of teaching goes back to my first job after graduating college—teaching sixth grade. It's very different than coaching business leaders, because in the sixth grade your job is to save everyone and move them on to seventh grade. In business you must accept that you can teach, but you cannot save everyone. I am willing to coach anyone on my leadership team as long as I still believe in him or her. I do have one absolute, and that is my values. If you don't share my values, you can't play on my team.

So now, almost a year into my assignment, I still did not have a leader in this all-important position. I decided to reach down into the organization, promoting a guy who had already demonstrated a talent for leadership and had deep organizational knowledge: Bill Mixon. The promotion was at first in an acting capacity. Bill had always been a sales guy, but he had worked hard to understand the service business. I saw that he had all the attributes I look for in a leader: communication skills, teamwork, energy, empowerment, and everything that Karen and I have discussed in this chapter. So I gave him a "trial by fire" to earn the job. He earned the role of service leader, which was, in my mind, never a risk but certainly a big stretch assignment much like those I had obtained several times in my career. **Good transformational leaders pay it forward.**

As it turned out, I was right about Bill. He did an outstanding job leading an organization of 3,500 employees with an operating budget of more than $600 million. Bill did such a good job that, when I moved on to USIS and saw the problems in our Investigative Services Division, I asked him to become divisional president, and he accepted. As mentioned previously, I hired John Moore to join me as operations VP, and I also brought in a bright young IT leader named James Choi, whom I had worked with at Philips. At that time, USIS had few clearly defined processes and a minimal IT department, and both John and James did a great job driving the company to a whole new level in those areas.

My decision to bring in James as Chief Information Officer, which was a huge stretch assignment of at least a two-level jump, was due to the technology that he and a small "skunk works" team created in Southern California to give our Philips Medical Systems sales and service business a unique operating platform. (See three documents on this work on pages 190-191 in the Appendix.) My message is this: Find change leaders, take a risk on them, and drive real innovation. Continuing to pay it forward, here was my opportunity to be James's Bill Fenoglio.

The fourth proven leader I brought in to USIS early on was Karen Query, who had helped me as a consultant with the HR side of integrating Philips. She played a similar role as a consultant at USIS, helping the in-house HR folks to enact and integrate the many new processes and roles that I expected of my HR team.

John and Bill are still with USIS as I write this, and those two leaders have driven as much process and productivity improvement as anyone I have ever worked with. John continues in his role leading process improvement, and my old foxhole buddy is comfortable in that role as he edges toward retirement. Bill, however, is substantially younger than John or I, and he is still on the rise. I'm proud to say that he is now president and CEO of four businesses supporting the federal government. Bill is now a CEO reporting to a CEO—just as I was at GE IT Systems and Philips—and he's leading an organization about the size of the total USIS business when I first took over as CEO.

As you can tell, I consider Bill a huge success story of reaching into an organization and finding a diamond in the rough. I've asked him to share his thoughts about how he kept himself on my radar, and how I helped him develop into the leader he is today.

Bill Mixon

"As vice president of sales operations, I was responsible for all awards and recognition throughout the company, and that gave me a lot of early exposure to Randy, first at the Hawaii event and continuing throughout the following year—because the CEO was ultimately involved in the awards. I also worked with Randy on his presentations to his boss and the Dutch corporate leadership. I had been with Philips for nine years when Randy arrived, so I knew quite a bit about the business and would advise him on his presentations and other communication activities. A tip for any young, ambitious leader: Look for opportunities to gain exposure to the CEO through special projects.

"As Randy mentioned, I was the only non-senior-staff person who attended the Marriot sessions. In part, I was there because Randy trusted me, and it's good to have people you trust during the sequestering process. I was also there to support my boss, the vice president of sales. Together we had already spent a lot of time building the integration model. Finally, I was involved in all the packaging and communication of the recommendations, so that gave me more exposure to the CEO.

"Randy also mentioned that I traveled with him across the country for the town halls and business reviews, and this really cemented our relationship. Nothing like going on the road with your boss, or in this case, your boss's boss, to find out about him as a person and a leader, give him an opportunity to find out about you, and really learn how he thinks and acts.

"So over time, Randy's trust in me grew and, either consciously or subconsciously, he saw me as a second-tier guy who had the potential to step up when appropriate. I was also part of his extended staff, so I was in on extended staff meetings, which is another unique tool that Randy used to surround himself with people and opinions beyond his immediate staff.

"When Randy promoted me to vice president of customer service, he understood that I didn't know much about running a medical services business. But he knew that I had an affinity for leadership, and, after two failed leaders, the service business desperately needed good leadership. We had good regional field vice-presidents who knew their jobs. We also had an excellent chief financial officer (CFO), a South African guy named Andre Oberholzer, who is my CFO at USIS today. I drove a performance-based orientation, but for the most part these and other leaders just needed to be listened to and supported to do their jobs—and our performance took off. We knocked the transformational cover off the ball for two years in a row, following the lead of Randy and others who shared service knowledge and the whole transforming process.

"Naturally, I appreciate what Randy did for me at Philips, and the opportunity he gave me at USIS. I didn't know anything about background investigations when I arrived, but after the Philips experience, I knew how to run a service business, and you can apply the same principles to any service business. It's just a matter of gaining practical skills that apply to specific services. I can honestly say that we have transformed the investigative services division in the last four years. I'm proud to be leading an extraordinary and dedicated team."

※ ※ ※ ※

I thank Bill for his comments. I'm sure you can tell from his thoughts on leadership why I chose him for the job. I didn't have to teach Bill how to work hard and persevere; I just had to coach him on some specific aspects of the medical services business, and how to think and act as a transformational leader.

Letting leaders go

So far in this chapter, I've shared my experience of encountering three talented leaders who became part of my "Dream Team." Those are the good stories, but there's another side, too: knowing when you have to let someone go. One of a transformational leader's most important responsibilities when you first take over an organization is to determine whether or not you have the right senior-leadership talent. If not, you have to bring in the right senior leaders or you will lose credibility with the employees. Most employees know poor leadership when they experience it, whether it's their immediate supervisor or the senior leader of their organization, and they are watching closely to see if you'll recognize and deal with it.

As I explained earlier, USIS had three divisions when I first arrived. The smallest and newest was the Commercial Services Division (CSD), headquartered in Tulsa, Oklahoma. They specialized in pre-employment screening for the commercial business world: services like employment history, criminal records checks, department of motor vehicles (DMV) history, and résumé verification. The CSD business was and still is heavily driven by computer technology with some telephone verifications. While the federal government is concerned with quality and depth as well as price, the commercial background-screening world is almost entirely driven by price. It's a very competitive market with a huge upside—an estimated \$2 billion/year—and it was a question of how much market share CSD could win. Unfortunately, it wasn't winning as much as it should have won.

I spent my first six weeks focusing on ISD. That was our biggest earnings improvement opportunity and had to be tackled first. So it wasn't until mid-April that I first visited the Tulsa headquarters. Unlike the other USIS divisions, most of the 500+ CSD employees worked at one site, so I expected to accomplish a lot in this visit and was scheduled to stay for a whole week. The story I'd like to share with you now is the complete opposite of the John, Karen, and Bill stories.

The CSD president had worked as VP of sales for one of CSD's top competitors, ChoicePoint. He had been hired shortly after CSD's acquisition build-up, so he had been there more than a year. I had only met him briefly for breakfast in Atlanta prior to joining USIS. My VP of human resources at that time, Susan Rogers, accompanied us, and we took off Monday morning from Atlanta. We flew first class, so it would be easier to talk and debrief on the way to Tulsa. Susan took the inside seat, with me in the aisle seat and the divisional president in the aisle seat opposite me. For this story, let's call him Bob.

No sooner had the plane taken off than Bob fell asleep and slept all the way to Tulsa! I was astonished. I've seen a lot of strange things in my business career, but I have never seen a senior leader fall asleep during his first opportunity to really talk with the new CEO. As strange as it was, it got stranger from there.

I spent the rest of Monday and all of Tuesday through Thursday gathering information and insight from every level of the organization, from Bob's senior staff to hourly front-line employees. It quickly became clear that there were serious problems in Tulsa and most reflected a lack of leadership from Bob. It didn't help that he continued to live in Atlanta, thinking he could run the company spending about three days a week in Tulsa. I figured out his schedule by analyzing his expense reports. I am nothing if not persistent.

Bob continued to act strangely toward me, missing a scheduled meeting and failing to ask a single question throughout the week about me, my style, or my expectations. Believe me, I'm not looking for extra attention. However, as I've emphasized many times throughout this book, a transformational team is driven first and foremost by communication, and all good communication is two-way. If I'm the new CEO and one of my senior leaders doesn't want to know anything about me, then I know we have a problem.

Finally, on Friday morning, I presented Bob with a list of my concerns. A transformational leader must always be assessing his leaders, and that assessment should be ongoing. This was a key moment for Bob, his first assessment from his new CEO, but he just didn't get it. I still have the list of concerns I presented, and I'd like to share them to give you an idea of just what a mess the business was under his leadership:

- Lack of knowledge about financial details;
- Lack of a plan to drive financial objectives;
- Lack of engagement with the broad Tulsa team;
- A controlling leadership style;
- Limited team dynamics...too sales organization oriented;
- Lack of operating protocols;
- No real integration of the former businesses;
- Lack of openness in his communication style;
- Failure to pull the team together.

I discussed these issues with Bob and told him, "You've got two weeks to put together an action plan and get back to me, and 60 days to make significant progress in implementing your plan."

When we were scheduled to discuss these issues further, Bob quietly left the office, left his rental car in the parking lot, and had a sales associate drive him to the airport. Before he got on his plane, he called John Clark, my operating partner at Welsh, Carson, Anderson & Stowe, the private equity firm that owned USIS at that time and for whom I work today. He told John I was trying to destroy him and the Tulsa operation.

John called me late Friday afternoon, and I explained what had just happened. I was on strong footing, because Welsh Carson had hired me to do exactly what I was doing: build a senior leadership team that could help me transform USIS into a growing and more profitable business. In order to build that team, I had to learn about the senior leaders I had inherited and decide who were the keepers and who had to leave. I told John what had just happened, and he said, "Fine. I won't take his calls. Do what you have to do."

I fired Bob, and though I don't like to fire people, that one didn't hurt a bit. The most important aspect of this change was the support and admiration I received from so many folks in CSD who knew the change was critical to a better future.

Bob was a classic case of quickly discovering that one of your senior leaders cannot be part of your transformational team. Sometimes, it's not that easy to tell, and it's seldom as easy to fire someone. It's even tougher when you hire a leader you really believe in, give that leader as many chances and as much coaching as you can, and then still have to fire him or her. I have a number of those stories from throughout my career, but one of the most pointed and poignant for me remains the story of the guy I hired to replace Bob. Let's call him Chris.

Like Bob, Chris had been a sales leader at ChoicePoint, but the similarity ended there. Chris is an open, friendly person, with the utmost integrity, generosity, and a strong social conscience. Among his greatest accomplishments at CSD was creating a thriving, dynamic culture of community service.

This is something that I believe in strongly, and I made it a part of our vision at USIS. I believe if we are fortunate enough to make our living in a community, we should give back to that community. Community service not only helps the community; it also helps the people who volunteer their service to feel good about themselves. It builds camaraderie and teamwork both inside and outside the office. Chris didn't just encourage his employees to give back to the community; he gave generously of his own time, serving as chairman of the Tulsa Juvenile Diabetes fundraiser and taking on other high-profile volunteer responsibilities.

Chris is a hard guy not to like, and people responded to him. He increased communication activity and worked with Paul on a bi-monthly newsletter. He understood the integration problems and took positive steps to meet them. In the end, however, I felt he did not act aggressively in pursuing his financial objectives. I needed a different leader in Tulsa, and Chris and I came to the conclusion that he and his family should return to the East Coast. It's never fun to select and support a new senior leader and once again make a change within a couple of years, but it's one more component of a transformational leader's job.

Chris's case demonstrates something I have learned throughout my career: A successful leader can't just have some of the attributes you are looking for; he or she must have *all* the attributes. It's a constant battle to build the right transformational team at any given time. Change is relentless and constant, and the leadership team has to change as necessary to achieve high-end performance.

New Manager Assimilation

I'd like to end this chapter by sharing a leadership exercise that I learned at GE and first used in Mexico in 1984. I also used it to great effect at most of my other GE jobs, and at Philips and USIS. It's called New Manger Assimilation. The intent of this exercise is to quickly bridge the communication and personal-knowledge gap between a leader and his direct reports. Without this exercise it might take as long as six months for the leader and staff to really get to know each other. This helps break down the unknowns between you and your staff, greatly accelerating the process.

This exercise—along with most of the insights I share in the book—is not limited to a CEO. Any leader with a staff can use it, whether in the business world or in another type of organization. Both the leader and the staff must trust whoever facilitates the process. I have generally used HR leaders as facilitators. For example, a talented HR leader named Ron Hancock facilitated the New Manager Assimilation at GE Medical Systems, Karen Query facilitated at Philips, and both Karen and Ron Hancock facilitated at USIS.

The exercise is very simple and straightforward. The staff gathers in a room with the facilitator and without the top leader present. You can do this onsite or offsite. Either way, the senior staff and leader are taking a day out of their lives to get to know each other. The facilitator asks the staff to answer four questions, and writes the answers on white boards, with the responders remaining anonymous to the leader. So, as long as everyone trusts the facilitator, they should all feel comfortable completing this exercise. Here are the four questions. I'll use my name as an example.

1) What do you know about Randy Dobbs?

2) What do you want to know about Randy Dobbs?

3) What should Randy know about you?

4) What are the problems/issues that face our organization and face us as a team?

If you consider these questions, you'll see that they are in descending order of seriousness and risk. Question 1 is kind of fun and without risk. No one is expected to know anything in particular at this point, so it just gets the communication flowing. Question 2 gathers information, still not too risky. Question 3 is more serious, testing the water, giving the staff the opportunity to define themselves in both a personal and business context. The fact that the staff hears everyone else's response helps solidify teamwork. Finally, Question 4 is the real kicker. The staff can ask for what they believe they need and position themselves for the changes ahead.

I went back to my records from over the years and compiled some of the responses I've received to these four questions. They're fun and interesting. If you'd like to read them, you'll find them in the Appendix, p. 178.

When the staff has provided its input, the leader enters the room, and the facilitator presents the anonymous questions and answers. The leader then has an opportunity to respond. The fact that the first question is light, followed by progressively more serious ones, allows the leader to start with some light, funny comebacks, and move on from there. For example, when they say I'm tall (6'6"), I'll say, "Not by NBA standards," and that always gets a laugh. You want to start with that kind of response to put everyone at ease. Then you can move into addressing the serious business concerns.

Having gone through this exercise multiple times, I can tell you it is enlightening for the leader; and, from the feedback I've gotten, it's also enlightening for the staff. You can see from the responses in the Appendix where I got some of my introductory-presentation ideas I included in chapter 4. For example, when asked by the senior staff about my pet peeves, I thought that was a good issue to address in my introductory presentations to the whole organization.

The New Manager Assimilation should be conducted as soon as possible, given the specific circumstances. At GE Medical Systems we worked this exercise after my first week on the job. More typically, it will take place sometime during the first month or two. Although this exercise is designed to break the initial barriers between a leader and his staff, it is sometimes a good idea to repeat it. After about two years at USIS, I brought in a new, experienced HR leader named Dave Whitmore. After doing his own initial fact-finding, Dave told me that some of the leaders were less than comfortable with my style, and didn't feel they really knew me well enough. So we decided to run the exercise again, and it proved helpful in creating a stronger team direction just months before we began the process of selling the company.

I hope you can see how important building, mentoring, and constantly evaluating the right team is to your transformational success. However, in the next chapter you will find that it takes vision, perseverance, and commitment to really launch that right team in the right direction. How many bright but stubborn people have you seen drive by their destination, lacking a vision for where they were really going?

CHAPTER 8

Set the Vision and Create Buy-in

If you've ever taken high-school chemistry, you should know what a catalyst is. Even if you haven't taken chemistry, I'm sure you've encountered the word in other contexts. In the four previous chapters, I've shared many ingredients of the Secret Sauce that will enable you to transform virtually any organization. Every ingredient in the Sauce is essential, but there is one ingredient that acts as a catalyst for the others, and that's the subject of this chapter. Before I discuss that ingredient, I'd like to share the critical definition of "catalyst" from the Merriam Webster online dictionary:

> ...an agent that provokes or speeds significant change or action.

The Secret Sauce's catalyst is vision. A successful transformational leader must create and communicate a vision that will achieve the change necessary to drive the organization—from your senior leaders on down—to embrace it, make it their own, and commit to change around that vision. To accomplish this, you must convert followers into leaders and transform leaders into agents of change.

At USIS, for example, under the previous command-and-control style of leadership, district managers did what they were told. I took a very different approach, explaining to the district managers, who are comparable to leaders in similar situations in every business: "You can't just follow me. You have to listen to what I share with you about where we need to go and help me get there."

That offered the district managers an opportunity to embrace the vision and make it their own. Those who did, stayed. Some went on to great success and significant promotions, while those who failed to embrace the vision simply had to leave. I have often used my own version of an old phrase: The train is leaving the station; you either get on the train or you're left at the station.

Some talented second-tier leaders were working at USIS when I got there, people like those who shared their perspectives on the Marriott experiences. They were already leaders, but quiet performers. I labored to turn them into agents of change, and they embraced that role as eagerly as they embraced the vision. As a transformational leader, you always must look for those hungry-to-grow leaders you can turn into agents of change.

This goes back to the chart I shared in Chapter 4, demonstrating the difference between a manager and a leader. Managing means being in charge. A manager masters routine. Leading means to influence, to guide, to create actions and opinions. **Leaders drive vision and attention to that vision.**

Even early on, after gaining only limited knowledge about the details, effective leaders must create a vision exposing potential organizational opportunities. To illustrate this, I'd like to share the last slide from my introductory presentation at USIS. I used the same basic slide at several other businesses, because the fundamentals are the same—it just needs minor adjustments for the specific business.

I did not include this with the other slides in Chapter 4, because it takes the discussion in a whole new direction. All of the other slides relate to introducing myself, my style, and my belief in leadership versus management. This slide begins to set the vision. I don't give this slide much time in my presentations; I just throw it up there at the end and introduce it almost apologetically, saying something like, "I've just begun to learn about this organization, so I don't know all the details, but here's my view of what we have to do in this business if we want to succeed." Then I flash this slide on the screen:

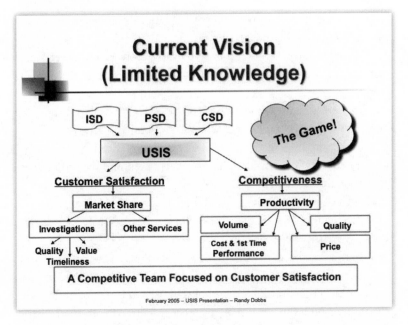

As you can see, this chart could apply to any business. Feel free to use it and adapt it however you wish. I didn't create this model; I first learned it in GE Medical Systems and utilized it in my later assignments. Customer satisfaction and competitiveness form the heart and soul of every successful business. Retaining and gaining market share has, at its heart, strong customer satisfaction, while productivity is the lifeblood of competitiveness—pure and simple.

No matter what the product or service, productivity is driven by increasing volume, improving quality, maximizing price, controlling cost, and achieving first-time performance. At the USIS Investigative Services Division, we had a service-specific problem with first-time quality and output of our investigations. We had the same fundamental problem with our refrigerator motors at the GE Motors plant in Jonesboro, Arkansas, when I got my first big job as manager of quality control. I shared with you in Chapter 3 how, on my first day on the job, our biggest customer, GE Appliances, rejected more than 40,000 motors because of quality issues. When I arrived at USIS more than 25 years later, our biggest customer, the U.S. Office of Personnel Management (OPM), was far too unhappy with our output and quality—and a much larger number of investigations that OPM didn't even see were rejected by our internal quality review process.

No matter what your product or service, every customer wants quality, timeliness, and value. These are universal truths in the business world.

So there isn't anything startling or creative in this chart—though it does reflect many years of experience—but here's the surprise: When I put this chart on the screen in town hall meetings with USIS investigators, a new, brief but strong, level of focus poured into the room. These smart, dedicated, and well-trained people had never been invited to share in a common business vision. They had been told what to do, and told they had to do it in the interests of national security and because their job security depended on it.

The national security emphasis was absolutely true, and everyone has to do their job well in order to keep it, but the idea of making them a part of the vision introduced a whole new dynamic. I was sharing with the investigators the same thought process I shared with their district managers and my senior leaders: "I'm going to show you where we have to go, but I need your help to get there." This represented for them a new level of conversation and openness about business needs.

I didn't keep the chart up for long or talk too much about it, because it was barely the beginning of a vision. Yet just the fact that I presented that beginning and invited them to share it with me signaled a start of our one-team journey.

Two weeks before I began the job, I showed the same set of slides with this same chart to the senior and second-tier leaders I would soon inherit. It was at a staff meeting held in Atlanta by my predecessor, Phil Harper. I later showed the chart and the other slides to many other employees throughout the business from ISD Support Services to our other two divisions, Professional Services and Commercial Services.

Here is an interesting psychological aspect of the Secret Sauce: I am willing to bet that, if you asked the employees and leaders who sat in on these meetings whether Randy Dobbs set a vision for them from the start, most of them would say, "No, he just told us a lot about himself." In fact, I was planting the vision's seed, whether they recognized it or not.

Empowering employees to make the vision a reality

The leader's next step is this: Direct and empower the employees to translate the vision into reality. Obviously, different employees have different jobs and different responsibilities in relation to the vision. The job of a leader like Bill Mixon or Mike Santelli to translate the vision is very different than an investigator's job. Investigators had a responsibility to do better, timelier, high-quality investigations. We had to give the investigators the right tools to accomplish this, but it remained their responsibility to take those tools and make their part of the vision a reality.

The reason Welsh Carson engaged me as CEO of USIS was to provide a bridge from the present to the future. If you think about it, that's what every leader is tasked to do, no matter what size the organization. If I had just gone in and created a new communication process, if I had just changed the senior staff, if I had just sent people to the Marriott and asked them to tell me what was wrong, then I wasn't really creating a bridge. I was putting a lot of tools in place, but that's not enough.

I'll stay with USIS as an example for most of this chapter, because it was my most recent assignment as a leader, and in some ways illustrates the fundamentals of this process better than any other job I've had; however, the same process has stood at the center of all my transformational roles.

After I completed my town hall meetings, received the report from the Marriott session, and began to hire a new senior staff, I went to Boyers, Pennsylvania, to meet with Kathy Dillaman, deputy associate director of OPM, USIS's largest customer. Kathy had direct responsibility for all OPM investigations, and neither Kathy nor OPM in general were happy with our performance at that time—the single-biggest threat to USIS's future. If we lost OPM as a customer, thousands of people would lose their jobs, and it is questionable whether the business would have survived. So I sat down with Kathy and worked to understand exactly what OPM saw as USIS's shortcomings, and what was most critical for us to address on a priority basis. What surfaced from this meeting was no surprise, and two key points became our mantra: 1) decrease the backlog of old, unfinished cases, and 2) improve our first-time throughput.

One key point I will share more about later is the importance of focusing on your business from a customer perspective. If you can't humble yourself, be willing to hear the bad news, and listen constructively to your customer, you simply cannot be a transformational leader, no matter how well you do the other things I've shared so far.

After that meeting, I began to set an agenda and get everyone in ISD focused on OPM. I didn't show that preliminary vision slide any more or talk about customer satisfaction in the abstract. I was working the customer satisfaction side of the vision by creating attention around what our customer wanted: reduction of backlog and improved first-time throughput. Once we had our agenda based on our vision, then we could start working toward results.

Although I always emphasize moving forward, you can only have a clear vision by understanding the past. USIS did some things very well before I got there, just as Philips and GE Medical Systems had done some things very well. So you have to understand that past and what was good about it. However, you have to look at the present and determine actions the business needs to move to the next level. **The reason for underperformance in most businesses—and most organizations outside the business world—is because they are stuck in the past.**

When I arrived at USIS in 2005, the company operated just as when it was first privatized in 1996 with about 300 investigators and 638 total employees. Now we had 3,000 investigators and about 7,000 total employees. We also had new customers, new services, and two divisions that didn't exist in 1996. The world of security services had changed, too, with new pressure from Congress to accelerate the security clearance process, new needs for our other professional services in places like Iraq and Afghanistan, and a new emphasis on pre-employment screening in the commercial business world.

So the company had grown and the marketplace had changed dramatically. Yet for all its growth, USIS had remained operationally the same for nine years—a lifetime in the modern business world. My job was to understand the past and present a clear vision for the future.

That's what every transformational leader must do. We don't have a crystal ball, but we have to work as hard as we can to see the opportunities and challenges that lie ahead, determine how best to realize those opportunities, meet the numerous challenges, and communicate the new vision and necessary actions to achieve it to the entire organization. That's what creating and implementing a vision is all about.

Vision is a choice of direction. A good leader has to possess hindsight, foresight, market vision, depth perception, and a time horizon. Some parts of the vision will be simple and quick to accomplish, some parts will be complex and long term, and some will require continuity with the past, while other parts will simply be wrong and will require modifications.

At USIS, the one constant has always been the national security mission: We serve our country; we focus on preventing 9/11 from happening again; we work to make the world a safer place. Phil Harper and his team did a great job of implanting this key part of the vision in the organization. I didn't have to work hard to keep it going, because the dedicated men and women who worked at USIS had already embraced it.

As a transformational leader, however, you have to determine what you need to retain for continuity with the past and what you need to radically transform. USIS required a number of radical changes, but my vision's most important component after six weeks on the job was radically transforming the investigators' experience. They had to be more empowered: measured by the work they did, not how far they drove every day. They had to take responsibility for their actions and the quality of their investigations. We had to give them new tools and technology to make their work more pleasant, more efficient, and more satisfying.

That's the genius of transformational leadership...the ability to challenge people with a vision that will excite them because of their own related opportunities to grow, improve, and drive their own future. I wasn't at USIS to tell those investigators their job wasn't important. It was and still is very important, and I was proud to be part of it. I wasn't there to tell them they weren't working hard enough or taking good enough notes, or that it was their fault we had all of these old cases. I was there to tell them that we can't win as a business unless the customers' satisfaction level improves dramatically, unless we become more competitive in all aspects of our performance, reduce the backlog, and improve our overall output.

Pulling the emotional lever

Persuasiveness is essential to creating a vision, because you must operate on the organization's emotional and spiritual heart. Real organizational change requires that level of deep penetration. In order to accomplish this, you don't drive home the vision; you drive home what *actions* must happen to make the vision a reality. You persuade your people that what they must do is best for themselves, their jobs, and their careers. There's no duplicity in this. A good transformational leader charts a vision that's best for everyone who is willing to embrace the vision as their own.

At USIS, my vision was pretty simple: 1) make the experience of working here much better; 2) do a better job for our customers; 3) be more competitive; 4) increase earnings; and 5) improve our investors' financial return. I expressed the first four parts of that vision very clearly. I was also clear about the ownership by a private equity firm and that its objective, whether selling the company or becoming publicly traded, could only happen by our success in the other four areas. That was the vision, but that's not what I emphasized day-in and day-out. Instead I emphasized the four key concepts that would make the vision a reality: People, Process, Productivity, and Growth.

I have explained the AskRandy communication program that first brought Paul and me together as collaborators. I used that program to drive People, Process, Productivity, and Growth into the organization's heart.

I did not introduce these concepts right away. First I had to open the lines of two-way communication, build and introduce my senior staff, share perspective from our largest customer, and send out other messages that set the table for a new, deeper level of communication. Then, during my fifth month on the job, I laid out these four concepts.

For the next two-and-a-half years, Paul and I pounded those four words so hard that not a single person at USIS could ever forget them or fail to understand what they meant. We focused on People in one AskRandy, on Process in the next, etc. When we had gone through all four, we started again, adding details around them and highlighting initiatives that helped our people, improved our processes, raised our productivity, or stimulated growth. We dealt with other subjects, too, but once I introduced those four words, I never allowed the focus to stray far from People, Process, Productivity, and Growth.

Of course, the AskRandy communication was not the only way I drove those words into the organization's heart. In the Investigative Services business, the most powerful drivers of change were the team leaders, discussed in Chapter 6. The team-leader program did not work very well at first for two reasons: 1) it took awhile to get the right people in those positions; 2) the team leaders did not fully embrace their new leadership task. We made great efforts to select and train these team leaders who were so integral to our future. I remained closely involved in this development process for hours on end until they really understood the changes we had to make. I worked hard to get emotional and spiritual buy-in from almost 170 investigators who had become new leaders. When they finally bought the vision and the path we had to take to achieve it, those 170 people went out and drove buy-in and change from almost 3,000 investigators.

To help drive home the vision and the path to achieve it, we held leadership conferences each year while I was at USIS. We based these conferences on the GE model, and they included about 300 top leaders from across the company. I could never meet with every single one of our employees individually, personally penetrating his or her heart and spirit; and it would have been difficult to work one-on-one with all 300 leaders.

I used the annual leadership conferences as a forum to really drive home my vision and the path to every one of those top leaders...a vehicle to communicate my vision through 300 zealots I had created, educated, and tasked with the job of taking the message back to the other 6,700 employees. Every conference ended with a strong speech: I asked those leaders to go back to their jobs, drive the message home to their own staffs, and push it on down the line.

In the Appendix, pp. 182-183, you'll find three charts from the FY 2008 Leadership Conference. The theme of the conference was built around the Fleetwood Mac song, "Don't Stop" with the lyric, "Don't stop thinking about tomorrow," and for USIS at that time, tomorrow was all about Growth. The first chart contains specifics that demonstrate how much we had changed in two years. Chart two emphasizes my four key words, with praise for People, Process, and Productivity, and a challenge for Growth. Chart three depicts a relatively simple Growth engine that I shamelessly stole from my old boss, Tom Dunham, at GE Medical Systems. I introduced this chart the previous year at the FY 2007 conference, and I brought it back again, because the engine had not yet produced the growth results that we needed.

Although the biggest challenge is growing emotional and spiritual buy-in from a broad employee base, you have to derive that same buy-in from your senior staff and closest advisors. I've shared Bill Mixon's great leadership qualities, but early on I battled to get that deep-level buy-in from him. He struggled with some things I knew he had to execute for ISD and USIS to succeed. So I kept pushing him. Sometimes I was harder on him than he deserved. Sometimes I just put my arm around him and coached him. Whatever I did, I mentored him until he saw what I saw, and agreed to take the path I knew he had to take. I did that with all my senior leaders, at USIS and at every leadership job I've had. The ones who couldn't see it, no matter how much I worked with them, had to find another job.

Putting this level of personal energy into the organization is exhausting, and there were times when I would tell Paul, "I just don't have the gas to do an AskRandy this week." We always did it anyway, and as we worked together to communicate some of the exciting initiatives in the business, I found a new energy I didn't even know I had. Top athletes talk about having another gear that kicks in when they're battling at the end of a match, and all professional athletes talk about how the crowd energizes them. It's a similar feeling in the business world. Many rewards come to a transformational leader, but one of the greatest is the energy your organization gives back in return for all you've given. That's why so many GE leaders exclaim that you must have massive energy and be an energizer for your organization to succeed.

Let's go back for a moment to the difference between a manager and a leader, only this time I'd like to say a few good things about managers. A manager looks at what actions to take in terms of the raw materials, technology, and human skills available to him or her. He or she thinks in terms of schedules and making critical dates—very important to any business. The people who can focus on them and keep them prioritized are good business people.

A leader has to master these aspects, as well; but the leaders who really transform organizations go way beyond this. They appeal on a deep emotional and spiritual level to workers' most fundamental human needs:

- Feeling important;
- Making a difference;
- Being part of something successful and worthwhile.

That's what we did at USIS and every business where I played a transformational role. We worked hard to make every employee feel important. We praised every employee for making a difference in the company and its service to our customers. We made every effort to convince every employee that he or she was part of a successful and worthwhile organization. In every one of my leadership positions, I made that emotional appeal to each and every employee.

It was easier to accomplish at a company like USIS, where even an entry-level employee could readily see our services were important in making the world a safer place. It was also relatively easy at GE Medical Systems and Philips, because the medical equipment we serviced improved lives every day.

It was more of a challenge to convince hundreds of Mexican teen-agers that the refrigerator motors we manufactured had this type of impact; but those kids wanted the same thing everyone else does, and we gave it to them. We made them feel important, congratulated them for making a difference at the plant, and convinced them that they were part of a successful and worthwhile organization. This last part was actually easier in Mexico, because those kids didn't have many other opportunities. It didn't take much convincing for them to see that the American giant, the General Electric Company, was a successful and worthwhile organization.

Most managers get things done. A manager can run an organization, but a manager will never take that organization to its pinnacle—because most managers do not make an emotional appeal. **Emotional appeal is integral to the Secret Sauce.** Very few business leaders think in terms of emotions. They think in terms of levers that must be pulled but miss the most powerful lever of all—the emotional appeal. To pull that lever requires a mastery of communication in every possible form.

Now perhaps you understand why I started the Secret Sauce section with communication. You must communicate many things during your journey as a transformational leader, but here's the objective you are always trying to achieve with that communication:

You have to touch people in the heart, soul, and spirit. You must give every ounce of energy you have to accomplish that goal. I've shared that I was so tired sometimes I couldn't imagine putting together another AskRandy, and that was the easiest communication. Ten weeks on the road for town halls and business evaluations took their toll, but leadership conferences were the greatest challenge of all. By the time I ended the conference with the CEO awards, I was so exhausted after three days of pumping up 300 leaders that I could barely walk off the stage. To continue my sports metaphors—great athletes talk about "leaving it all on the field," and that's exactly what you have to do in setting the vision and creating buy-in. Leave it all on the field or don't play the game.

(On pages 183-184, of the Appendix you will see how I closed that FY 2008 Leadership Conference with my commitment to personal action to improve my own Growth leadership. I then asked each of the 300 attendees to write and commit to their own 2008 Growth Plan.)

In closing, let's transition to my final thoughts on vision, and move toward wrapping this section on the Secret Sauce over the next two chapters. The next chapter will deal with the final aspect of putting all this work together: using this emotional energy and vision to create a new culture that will forever change the way a business thinks and acts. What could be more of a transformational high? You're creating and shaping a culture that will go beyond you as a leader of the business.

CHAPTER 9

Implementing the Vision
Creates Cultural Change

In the last five chapters, I've shared with you some of the Secret Sauce's more important ingredients that enable leaders to transform any organization, including two vital elements: setting the vision and creating buy-in.

Let's think about these as the ingredients for a transformational cake. You now have the ingredients necessary to create that cake and present an exciting end product. However, few people are attracted to even the best-baked cake without the tasty icing that really finishes it. The icing on the Transformational Leadership cake makes this a cake that can't be beat in the future...cultural change.

In many respects, cultural change is the best return on investment for a transformational team's senior leaders. You can communicate, get feedback from the organization, bring in the best senior leaders, and gain buy-in for your vision, but until the culture changes, you will not achieve lasting transformation. As the culture changes, the senior leadership will see the true transformation in the organization's power. You have to keep driving change, of course, because, as I have shared, change is never-ending. However, once the organization's fundamental culture begins to shift, the leaders no longer have to *drag* the organization into the future. The organization begins to *lead* the change into the future state.

In order to make an organization's vision work, you must engrain that vision in the people's hearts and minds. I will discuss three different ways you can drive a vision a little later in this chapter. For now, I want to emphasize this: The single most important factor in implementing and positioning a vision that drives true cultural change is to establish trust. **Trust is not given freely, and no leader can mandate trust. Trust, like respect, is earned.**

Paul and I relentlessly worked on our AskRandy messages to earn the USIS organization's trust. We chose every word, every sentence, every idea very carefully to establish trust in Randy Dobbs as a visionary leader. The vision was sound, but I also knew that vision was only the start of winning in the competitive business world; we could only realize true success through buy-in from those who had to do the work. The strongest and most significant level of buy-in is cultural change.

In the previous chapter, I discussed the challenge in balancing an appreciation for the organization's history and culture with my desired vision of the future. Understanding that existing culture is essential for a leader to establish trust. Every concerned employee must be convinced that the new leader understands the business's sacrifices, successes, and disappointments created in its current culture. When you exhibit that you understand and respect the past, most employees will begin to accept and trust your new, compelling vision. They will link the past to the future and embrace the necessary changes to succeed in creating a new cultural direction.

I am convinced there are two factors you must clearly address to fully gain the organization's trust in your vision and cultural direction. First, the vision must be clear, appealing, and doable. If you think back to the slide I shared in Chapter 8 that outlined my initial vision for USIS (and for any other business), it was crystal clear: Satisfy our customers and drive business competitiveness. It was also appealing—everyone in the room could see that satisfying the customers and becoming more competitive would make us a more successful business, and successful businesses can better ensure the future for their employees. Finally, it was a *doable* vision. There was nothing too intimidating, nothing insurmountable. In fact, when I presented that slide in town hall meetings, I always felt that the nodding heads in the audience were not just agreeing with me, but also indicative of many brains in the audience thinking, "Yeah, we can and need to accomplish this."

The second factor essential to implementing the vision is this: Your position as a leader must be just as clear as the vision, and your commitment to that vision must be unquestionable as the catalyst for cultural change. You could read through all 53 AskRandy messages and would never find a single word that suggests anything other than total commitment to my vision.

Once you establish trust, you can position the need for your vision with one or more of three different drivers:

- **Reactive**...We have to change our business to survive. In the business world, you must react to changing needs or the business most likely fails.

- **A Change in the Environment**...This can be external or internal. For example, at USIS, a significant external change was the increased security requirements after 9/11. A significant internal change at all three firms—GE Capital IT Systems, Philips Medical Systems North America, and USIS—was investor demand for significantly improved earnings.

- **New Market Mandates**...At both GE Medical Systems and Philips, the new market mandate was that great service on expensive medical equipment would drive sales and earnings more than new technology or equipment. Customers were demanding equipment uptime and less performance issues more than increased equipment functionality.

As you can guess, looking at the three bullet points above, the best positioning for a transformational team is to consider all three of these drivers. Use them all to show how your vision is right and must be embraced for future success. This is the foundation of why the culture must change.

As you begin to call on the trust you've earned and work to position your vision, lessons are unleashed and transformational leadership really begins to reap multiple benefits. You can establish and define a shared-values commitment that uniquely reveals many aspects of your organization's direction—a blueprint that will create the culture of tomorrow.

In every organization I have transformed, we distilled those shared values down to one piece of paper. It included our Vision Statement, our Mission Statement, and our Supporting Strategies. In this context, the word "vision" takes on a different meaning than the vision I have been discussing so far—the vision that a transformational leader creates based on his or her insight into the organization and future goals. That's the vision that drives business cultural change, moving the business into a new way of thinking, acting, and performing.

A Vision Statement is different. Along with the Mission Statement and Supporting Strategies, it is the first key component of the shared values. We ask everyone in the organization to commit to these new cultural values that will in turn drive future business success. I'm often asked what the difference is between a Vision Statement and a Mission Statement, and how the Supporting Strategies fit into the picture. Here's my simple, straightforward explanation:

- A **Vision Statement** captures where an organization wants to go. By its nature, a Vision Statement is futuristic. It may take quite some time to achieve, but it is imperative that everyone in the organization sets their sights on this Vision. They must work together to drive toward it as a reality, although it may take years to achieve. This is the foundation for the new culture.

- A **Mission Statement** describes "how" the organization will achieve the Vision over time.

- The **Supporting Strategies** are the building blocks that support the Mission.

As I mentioned, my senior staff and I have defined these values for multiple organizations throughout my career. However, my most recent assignment at USIS allowed me and my leadership team greater freedom in redefining the business. Unlike my assignments at GE or Philips, USIS was a standalone organization that did not have to align with a larger corporate culture. We had to respect the past, of course, but we were free to be more creative in defining and changing our future business direction.

Throughout this book, I have shared helpful documents that I felt you could adapt to your own business needs. I'd like to share the values we defined for USIS in November 2005, after I had been on the job for nine months. As I was writing this, it struck me that nine months is the time it takes for a child to grow in the mother's womb, and that's a pretty good metaphor for the "gestation period" necessary to develop and define an organization's set of shared values. Some of these values are specific to the USIS business, while others might apply to any business. Taken together, they should help you understand how to put together a set of shared values that work together to define cultural change.

Vision Statement

To be the premier provider of knowledge-based security solutions, ensuring a safer future today.

Mission Statement

To deliver best-in-class people, processes, and technology in partnership with our diverse customer base, creating value for shareholders, employees, and community.

Supporting Strategies

- **Integrity:** Establish a USIS culture of unconditional daily compliance.

- **People:** Inspire and motivate everyone to become the best they can be; reward success and excellence.

- **Process:** Create a business culture that constantly challenges the status quo to find smarter, more efficient ways of working.

- **Growth:** Make sustained, profitable growth the lifeblood of the business through a relentless focus on value-added customer solutions.

- **Customers:** Deliver value-added solutions that enhance the success of our clients in serving their customers and achieving their missions.

- **Community:** Make a difference where we live as well as work; be a recognized partner in the community.

You can readily see how brief, clear, and integrated these shared values are. They are so brief, we printed them on both sides of a business card, and gave a card to every employee to carry in his or her wallet. I don't know how many of the employees actually read these cards, but I do know we did everything we could to give this new cultural direction visibility to all. I emphasized these values in AskRandy messages, my senior staff emphasized them in their own newsletters and other communications, and we printed posters that we hung in every office. (You can find the posters in the Appendix, pages 180-181.)

This exercise and end product facilitated a unique opportunity to develop a new time and space for USIS, and a new brand logo for the marketplace. The old USIS "look" was developed at the time the company first privatized in 1996. My predecessor, Phil Harper, was acutely aware—and rightly so—that he had to move cautiously in breaking away from the federal government image, both for his initial single customer—OPM, the same agency out of which USIS developed—and for his initial employee base, almost all former OPM employees. He and his team developed a golden seal similar to the seals used by government agencies, and he prominently displayed bronze statues of eagles throughout the corporate offices. The corporate colors were an elegant green and gold, and the corporate logo a classic treatment of the letters "USIS" using those colors.

When I arrived nine years later, I clearly saw that the initial corporate brand had served its purpose and the company had grown beyond its federal government origins. Although OPM remained the largest customer for the Investigative Services Division, we now had two other divisions: the Professional Services Division, with contracts in the Middle East, Africa, Asia, and South America; and the Commercial Services Division, with some 30,000 customers in the commercial business world. So we had to create a new image that not only reflected a new present but also suggested a new and dynamic future.

The details are not important, but I will share a few key changes we made and the reasons we made them. First, we altered our corporate colors to red and black, colors we felt gave us a bolder, trustworthy, and in-control look. We chose new fonts for the same reason, and combined the colors and fonts in a new logo that set the letters "USIS" against a world map, with the tagline: "Insight, Intelligence, Integrity." We used all these components in a new website and marketing materials with an edgier look suggesting a company aiming toward the future, dedicated to creating a safer future today. (You can see grayscale versions of the old and new logos in the Ask-Randy messages in chapter 5, as well as in the Appendix, pp. 164-171.)

Now, you may wonder what colors, fonts, and logos have to do with culture change. I would answer that they are just as integral a component as the shared values I outlined. The "look" of an organization not only conveys a message to the customers, shareholders, and other constituents; it also constantly reminds employees that their organization has changed and will continue to change.

My successor as CEO of USIS, Mike Cherkasky, has subsequently changed the corporate name to Altegrity, and kept the well-known brand names of the three main businesses: USIS, HireRight, and Explore. I could not change the corporate name during my tenure, because the corporate culture was not yet ready for that. Believe me, plenty of people missed the old USIS look and logo, but they were far outnumbered by those who felt the new look represented the whole USIS and its future. I clearly saw that whatever I changed, all those changes had to be around the established USIS name to provide the necessary continuity with the past.

I knew I had to create a new corporate culture making change a given, without losing the focus on integrity. I emphasized change again and again in my communications, as well as by throwing change at the organization with our new shared value statements and new look. I emphasized change so much during my first nine months that, at our first leadership conference—the same conference where I unveiled the new values, logo, and look—I presented a pretty funny slide of myself as the "change monster." I threw several ugly change-monster dolls into the audience when I got the right answers to various questions about our cultural changes. That got a good laugh from the leaders at the conference, some of it nervous laughter of folks who knew they were on a thrill ride and weren't sure where it was going to take them. (See the Appendix, p. 179, for the change monster slide and a "growth monster" slide that followed it two years later.)

So I was a bridge from a corporate culture that emphasized the status quo to a culture making change a given in everything we did. Nothing went unquestioned or unchallenged. Nothing was done a certain way because that's the way it had always been done. As I've shared throughout this section on the Secret Sauce, the real force of cultural change came from within the organization, from the people who saw better ways to do their everyday jobs—not because they were expected to change, but to adapt to the cultural change.

My job was to set the table and set the standards. I had to be the "change monster." When I left USIS, every single person in the organization had accepted the fact that change had become, and always would be, an integral part of the business—which is exactly how I was taught to see the world at GE.

That was the cultural change that my staff and I created. That new culture allowed Mike Cherkasky to make his radical organizational changes in a very short time. I am no longer involved with USIS, so I don't know how those changes are working out. I do know that, just as Phil Harper was a bridge from the federal government past and I was a bridge from there to a culture of change, Mike is a bridge from the culture he inherited to a future perhaps only he sees today. My team and I created a new past for the organization, and Mike and his team are creating a new past every day.

None of these cultural changes can happen without a real deployment of self, the transformational leader's full commitment to the vision and the cultural change that vision will create. I've already discussed many attributes of a transformational leader, but I'd like to offer another list of any leader's character traits necessary at this cultural-change stage of the transformational process:

- **Know your strengths and weaknesses;**
- **Be willing to take risks;**
- **Establish and commit to both short and long-term objectives;**
- **Drive consistency and dependability;**
- **Be persistent...never give up.**

This last trait goes back to the second chapter, "If You Want to Win, Never Give Up," and I've illustrated the other attributes throughout the book. A transformational leader must possess these qualities to inspire his people to follow him passionately, and passion is a requisite for cultural change.

When you create a new culture, you are inspiring people to modify their core beliefs—who they are in the business. When I arrived at GE Medical Systems, the field staff had core beliefs about GE Medical Systems. The same goes for every transformational assignment I have undertaken, and the cultural change I have been describing at USIS is a perfect example.

People followed me into a new culture because being part of the new direction felt better than being left behind in the old world. In the previous chapter, I discussed the employees' emotional commitment to embrace the leader's vision. I believe the emotional commitment required to accept cultural change is even deeper, because it touches core values. Once an employee embraces those new core values, he or she has a new level of empowerment to change the organization.

A successful transformational leader must create a culture always ready to change. Even more important, it will always WANT to change as conditions require. A transformational leader's major goal is to stop pushing ideas out to employees, and inspire employees to want new ideas and pull those ideas into action. I have shared how I emphasized certain ideas again and again in my communications. This is pushing ideas out, and it is a necessary initial step in the transformational process.

Real cultural change ignites when the leader no longer has to push all the change out to the organization, because the organization wants change and pulls change toward them. At this point, the transformational leader becomes like an orchestra director, calling up the best in every asset of the business, and making decisions regarding who plays first violin, who plays second, and who is no longer adding to the orchestra.

So far in this chapter, I have shared many ideas and insights, showing how driving vision and buy-in facilitates cultural change. I have also shared some details of how I created a new culture of change at USIS. I would like to end by sharing how the culture changed at two very different organizations: the GE Motors maquiladora plant in Mexico and GE Medical Systems in the Southeastern United States.

Cultural change at GE Motors in Reynosa, Mexico

When I first arrived at the Reynosa plant, the culture I found was very typical of most maquiladora plants. The teenage workers viewed the leadership as "gods" from "el Norte," the North, who knew all the answers. Most of those kids had less than an eighth-grade education. Their only commitment to the business was to show up for work, do their job, have enough to eat, and help to provide basic essentials for themselves and their family. In other words, survival was the driver for these kids.

We worked very hard to provide our young workers with a sense of becoming part of something special that not only offered a way to feed their families, but also created an opportunity to achieve whatever they desired...the good old free-enterprise system. We allowed various factory work groups to elect their own team leaders, naming their teams with sports analogies or other things popular with young kids. They had a sense of being part of a real team within the larger organization of the plant. We promoted from within whenever possible, so everyone realized that the door to opportunity was always open.

We acknowledged their contributions in a variety of ways, a big cultural shock to them. When we first met our goal of manufacturing 50,000 motors per week, we had T-shirts printed with the message, "Gracias por su ayuda" ("Thank you for your help"). I handed them personally to every employee and shook hands with each of them. We changed our shift hours so they could go home in daylight, to avoid safety risks for our female employees, real dangers in our industrial park. We established a savings program, matching every peso they saved. Some of the most gratifying experiences of my business career were when those kids came in to see me with their whole family—father, mother, brothers, and sisters—and every one of them had new clothes and new shoes as a result of the savings program.

Think about these things as cultural change. They brought out the best in a bunch of teenagers living in a country that simply did not facilitate career aspirations, free-enterprise thinking, or personal relationships with the leader, and certainly didn't encourage savings.

By creating an atmosphere where the employees felt a part of a very different culture, we reduced turnover from 100% to 70%—still high by American standards, but a major improvement considering the Mexican culture and youth of the workforce. That 30% who stayed each year turned out to be a special group. Their level of commitment built a culture of performance, high quality, and productivity that did not exist before in our factory or our industrial park. During the fours years I worked in Reynosa, it was great to watch some of those kids grow, mature, and drive the cultural change.

Cultural change at GE Medical Systems, Southeastern region

GE Medical Systems was going through its own cultural transformation. When I joined the business, it was shifting from driving marketplace growth via new equipment technology to become a services business that would both realize financial gain from its large installed base and help differentiate the products driving new equipment sales. I joined a very strong team of service leaders who were recruited by

GE Medical Systems Services VP Jim DelMauro and subsequently led to even more significant accomplishments by Jim's successor, Tom Dunham.

GE Medical Systems was about as different from the maquiladora plant as two businesses could be, and I had to take a very different approach to cultural change. There the well-educated field engineers went out to work on high-end medical equipment. They went where they were assigned, and most were extremely good at their jobs and customer relations. However, they had little or no understanding of how the business worked, with limited knowledge of our financial results. For all they knew, we could have been going down the tubes financially. We weren't, but they didn't know that. More important—they didn't understand how their individual performance affected our business success, and why continued cost productivity was so important to our future.

For six years, I spent almost all my time on the road, getting to know as many of our employees as I could. I held town halls and performance reviews, consistently communicating the message that every employee, whether a district manager or a field engineer, had to take ownership of the business. I changed the district manager position from a paper pusher and scheduler to an empowered business leader, responsible for the success of his district and for building and growing modality teams with all the field engineers. (A modality team is a team focused on one type of equipment; for example, the X-ray machine team or the CAT scan team.)

We also empowered the field engineers to make their own decisions for the good of the business and the customers. We made one engineer in each location a modality team leader. This was quite different than the team leader program at USIS, discussed in Chapter 6, because the leaders did not have supervisory responsibilities, but they did coach, train, and mentor to improve their team's service performance.

Their biggest responsibility was to balance the need to add engineers with a growing installed base, thereby driving productivity and utilizing our new remote monitoring technology created and implemented at headquarters. For example, if the sales organization had the opportunity to sell two new CAT scan machines in a given area, we would first require the lead engineer of the area's CAT scan service team to help close the sale, and, once the sale was completed, to devise a plan covering the new installed base with little or no additional headcount. So, as the business progressed, the modality leaders—and most of the other engineers—understood the implications of our investments and the need to drive bottom-line growth. The cultural change was to convince our talented field engineers that they were competing for survival with other medical service providers like Siemens and Toshiba, not just competing with the management team over good-paying jobs in the future.

If this sounds similar to my approach with the investigators at USIS, you are absolutely right. The services were different, but the dynamics were exactly the same. The field employees who generate revenue must take ownership of their role and how their performance affects the business that provides them a livelihood.

In closing, I'd like to go back to this chapter's beginning, and emphasize cultural change as the icing on the cake, the reward for all the hard work by the transformational leader and his or her staff. This is a change you can see. If it is the right change, you will leave the business with a culture that will take it into the future, professionally facing whatever new challenges lie ahead. It's a change that can and should make you proud to be a transformational leader. However, this is not the ultimate measurement of a transformational leader. Turn the page and we will verify our ultimate measure of success.

CHAPTER 10

The Real Secret: Earnings!

When I was in high school, my vocational education teacher would always lecture for about 50 minutes of the 55-minute class and begin the last five minutes by saying, "I said all that to say this." Then he'd give us the key point. I remember that teacher and that remark as clearly as if it were yesterday. It's a good metaphor for what I've been doing so far in this book.

I have shared some core values at the heart of being a strong transformational leader. I have worked you through all the fundamental ingredients of the Secret Sauce, which will clearly give you the building blocks for your own transformational adventure. So, I said all of that to say this: Your Secret Sauce won't achieve that winning taste without focusing on and delivering sustained and improved financial results.

You may be viewed as a successful communicator, a strong team-builder, a thoughtful visionary, or a real cultural change agent, but all of those efforts echo as empty rhetoric if you don't produce the financial results your investors and your market demand. No one ever engaged me as a transformational leader to drive better communication, build a senior leadership team, create a vision, or change a culture. The only reason to engage any business transformational leader, including me, is to achieve the financial results!

Before we go on, let's discuss what the term "achieving financial results" really means. Perhaps you'll recall the quote from Jack Welch that I shared in Chapter 2 as I proceeded to take over a business losing $100 million per year net of operations: "Randy, there isn't a single GE shareholder who's enamored with revenue. All they care about is earnings."

Jack was a gifted visionary leader, but in this case he was just emphasizing a truth that every transformational business leader knows, whether he leads a publically traded business, a privately owned business, or an employee-owned business. At the end of the day, the chief financial result that every stakeholder cares about is earnings.

Revenue is critical, because it is an essential component of growing earnings, but, even without revenue, earnings are the final score. You can grow a company's revenue 1% or 100%, but if you have not grown earnings at the same rate or better, then you have missed a transformational leader's ultimate measurement. With or without revenue growth, a real transformational leader never lowers his or her objective: driving earnings growth faster than revenue growth.

Yes, there are times when revenue will grow faster than earnings—and there are good reasons for that—but in the long run it's all about earnings. You may recall the famous phrase that political consultant James Carville posted in Bill Clinton's campaign headquarters during his first presidential election: "The economy, stupid!" Carville was right. Whatever you may think of Bill Clinton, history tells us that his focus on the economy—an issue where Republicans usually held the high ground—helped him win the 1992 presidential election.

The same laser focus applies to our business world. I was originally going to title this chapter, "The Earnings, Stupid," but I didn't want to turn you off or insult anyone before you read the most critical chapter! This is essential to remember each time you develop and review your transformational action plan. It must always focus on driving improvement in earnings, with stretch objectives that many will believe are neither fair nor achievable.

I believe that everything I've shared so far maps the plan a leader needs in order to drive business transformation and, with this focus, drive financial results. However, implementing the Secret Sauce outlined in the last five chapters doesn't guarantee financial success. To achieve real transformational financial success you have to stay focused every day, every week, every month, and every quarter on how the transformations affect the bottom-line results. Without significant transformation of the financial results, you are simply not a successful transformational leader.

Financial results at the end of a quarter, six months, or a year glare like the scoreboard at the end of a sporting event—the numbers tell the story. They declare whether you and your business have won or lost...for you, your associates, and your investors.

Think about the key ingredients I've shared. Opening up two-way communication, beyond establishing yourself, will improve employee morale and drive personal ownership among the work force. These are significant accomplishments for all involved, but in the business world, the driving force for improving employee morale and establishing ownership remains this: You engage employees to help drive the business's financial success. This is true of every ingredient in the Secret Sauce. They are all critical to successful business transformation, but they are really the tools and processes I used to ultimately change each company's financial performance.

I could have improved the financial performance—and perhaps more quickly—by being a "slash and burn" leader, and I might have sustained performance for a time with CEO mandates. However, I believe I could not build sustained financial performance quarter after quarter, year after year, without transforming the organization through the steps I've outlined in the last six chapters.

I'd like to share with you the financial transformation in each of the three businesses I "fixed" financially. Each had very different financial challenges. So, taken together, I believe you will gain insight into how the Secret Sauce can culminate, transforming people, the organization, and—most important—financial performance.

GE Capital IT Solutions (ITS)

This was my first and most difficult transformational challenge as a CEO. GE Capital IT Solutions was a reseller of IT hardware and software, a successful market niche in the late '80s and '90s. The big information technology organizations such as IBM, Hewlett-Packard, and Compaq did not have sufficient sales resources to sell all their products directly to end-users. So they worked with resellers, who packaged the products as an IT solution and sold it to various end-user businesses. It's a very straightforward business model: the reseller buys the products from the hardware manufacturer or software developer, marks up the product to typically achieve a 10% margin, and then works to sell an ongoing service agreement.

GE liked this asset-lite business with a strong return on investment, so in the mid-'90s they bought a $2 billion reseller in Minneapolis. They retained the CEO and provided the funding to acquire more than 40 smaller resellers and technology-service businesses around the globe. The company grew in revenue from that original $2 billion business to more than $4 billion in North America—the business I was tasked to lead—and $7 billion globally. Here's the task I faced as the new CEO: The many North American acquisitions had never been properly integrated, and the North American business alone was losing $100 million annually on a run-rate basis—the GE Company's worst performing business.

That was the situation when Jack Welch gave me his speech about earnings versus revenue. As I shared earlier in the book, he also said something else to me at that time: "We're not going to fix this with more growth. Those days are over. Do what you have to do to make this business profitable." Everyone in GE Capital and most of the GE corporate leadership, including Jack, knew the business was gasping on life support. We would have to use every process and resource in the GE company to fix it.

I had served as executive vice president for global services at ITS for about 18 months before being promoted to CEO in 2000, so I had a clear view of what I had to do. As always, I began with honest communication. At my first town hall, I told the employees, "I don't know how many of you will have jobs when we are finished, but I do know that we have to fix this business or no one will have a GE job. It's my job to save as many jobs as possible, but I know we will be forced to eliminate many of the jobs that exist today. However, when we achieve profitability, the jobs remaining will be more secure than any job here today. I need your help as we make these tough changes. I can't do it alone."

My job, as in every transformational challenge, was to communicate and convince the employees to work with me in implementing my vision: to cut costs dramatically, eliminate locations/segments that could not be fixed, and eliminate customers who wouldn't accept price actions where we had built systemic losses by providing more support to product purchases than we had priced. As you will notice, I didn't bullshit or offer false hope of growth to fix the issues. My honest message during the town halls undoubtedly made many people uncomfortable. In general, however, the employees at IT Solutions welcomed me as a transformational leader who would work to keep the business alive. Your workers in the trenches know the truth, and this was the truth at ITS: it was screwed up, losing money, and headed downhill at breakneck speed.

I used every transformational tool that I have shared with you, working to fix that business. I also used the financial support of GE to spend money on the fixes. I did take dramatic and tough actions, reducing the headcount over a two-year period from 5,700 to 3,100.

More important I reduced the ratio of general and administrative (G&A; i.e., overhead) employees to those who were really applying labor for our customers' benefit from 66% G&A to 50% G&A. We did this through utilizing technology and digitizing processes, allowing us to significantly reduce the back-office staff. In addition, we outsourced some of our back-office jobs to India—a practice now standard in many businesses. I sold off several assets, implemented the price actions that allowed us to get rid of unprofitable customers, reduced our compensation, benefits, and overhead costs from $400 million to $222 million, and shifted our strategic focus to create a game plan to return to profitability.

Working together with my senior leadership, which we rebuilt much like at USIS, and the 3,100 employees who survived this transformation, we implemented that game plan. Over the same two-year period, the North American business went from losing more than $100 million annually on a run-rate basis to squeezing out a profit of around $12 million in 2001.

That $112 million swing led to the GE Turnaround Business of the Year Award for me and my European counterpart, who also lessened the losses in his business. We received the award in Boca Raton, Florida, at the annual GE top leadership conference in January 2002. Jeff Immelt, the new GE CEO, made the presentations. I'm sure you can imagine how good that felt after losing and then regaining my GE officer stripes.

Despite the accolade—or perhaps because of it—senior GE leadership told me that, while they appreciated what I had done, they weren't sure what to do with the business. Until they figured that out, I wasn't going anywhere else in the GE organization. The business was sold a few years later, but I was long gone by then.

I have already shared the rest of the story of why I left GE for Philips. For now I want to emphasize three points:

- For all my success in turning the business around, my three-year tenure at GE Capital IT Solutions was one of the most painful and trying business experiences of my life. It's no fun going to work every day in a business that the parent company disdains, knowing you have to fire employees, shoot customers, and sell off assets...while also knowing that when the job is done you and your business will gain no love or appreciation as part of the company's future. I was the guy who had to keep a stiff upper lip as we did what had to be done—tying a tourniquet on the business, cutting every cost we could, and bringing it back to life. I was proud of our success, but I never felt the joy of victory. As they say down South, "You can put lipstick on this pig, but it's still a pig." That's how GE looked at us.

- I never could have turned that business around without following every step of the Secret Sauce roadmap for a transformational leader and having some key folks help me. As I assumed the role of CEO, I was assigned a top-notch cost-oriented CFO named Ron Collins. He was both my partner and my confidant as we worked though this painful situation for two years. I developed and used the Secret Sauce in leadership positions before becoming the IT Solutions CEO, but this overall experience proved my greatest business challenge. I found, without a doubt, that the Secret Sauce would work for any business, even one barely hanging on to life.

- I grew earnings by <u>reducing</u> revenue by more than $2 billion! That's what Jack meant when he said we weren't going to fix this problem with growth. He was willing to give up revenue to improve earnings, and that's exactly what I had to do.

This brings us back to this chapter's introduction. To be a successful transformational leader, you have to drive earnings results. Sometimes you need to increase revenue to increase earnings, sometimes revenue might stay roughly the same, and sometimes you have to reduce revenue. It depends on the business situation. However, whatever the situation, you must always keep your eye on the earnings objective, and create and work your game plan to achieve that goal. Earnings are literally the bottom line in a business story, so important that we use the term "bottom line" as a metaphor for the most important result in any endeavor.

Philips Medical Systems North America

As I shared in chapter 6, I had three offers for leadership positions after leaving GE. I chose the North American CEO position at Philips Medical Systems because I knew the medical systems market from my GE Medical Systems experience and enjoyed working in that kind of growth-oriented environment. Also, I knew that Philips' strong research and development had resulted in leading technology. I believed their customers, especially in the X-ray arena, had strong allegiance to their product and service team. I had the opportunity to interview with Philips Medical Systems' global leader, a smart guy from Finland named Jouko Karvinen. Although I was CEO of Philips Medical Systems North America, Jouko was my boss, just as I had a boss at GE Capital IT Solutions.

In our first meeting, Jouko explained his view of the leadership challenge facing me. He told me that Philips Medical Systems North America was a strong business in the world's largest imaging technology marketplace. The Netherlands-based Philips Corporation had recently invested approximately $5 billon to acquire four other medical services technology companies, a move to grow brand strength in North America beyond the X-ray business. "We've been working on the integration of these acquisitions for a year," he said, "and we're looking for a North American leader to take us to the next level in market share and growth."

My fundamental approach was to work the steps of the Secret Sauce, doing what Jouko tasked me to do—take the business to the next level. I had to quickly evaluate the business's financial performance and the integration process. As I have discussed in previous chapters, I was shocked at the lack of real integration, quickly realizing that, to create *one* Philips in North America, I would have to eliminate significant structural barriers and more than 250 leaders.

That was only the beginning. I had to convince the remaining leaders and employees to trust me, and to implement my vision for integrating the separate acquisitions into one Philips organization. I had to change the way sales and service were geographically aligned, create joint measurements, and drive market ownership for team success. I had to change the way we thought about delivering service. I had to completely shift the thought process in sales and drive the idea of selling a solution rather than just a product or service. Most of our sales people focused far too much on selling their product specialty, whether it was ultrasound, CAT scans, MRIs, or nuclear medicine. They were rewarded for selling those products, but that process had to change. Last, our relationship with the product managers in Europe was adversarial, with more focus on who to blame for market issues rather than how to win and keep customers.

Philips had not shared any financial information with me until I officially came on board, because they knew I had worked at GE, a competitor in the medical systems market. When I analyzed the financial statements, I discovered that, despite the parent corporation's huge investment, Philips Medical Systems North America was routinely missing their numbers on all fronts. They were in much better shape than GE Capital IT Solutions had been, but a corporation can't make a $5 billion investment and have their business fall short of its financial goals. So my challenge at Philips quickly went from an integration issue to an earnings issue and a marketplace customer-growth issue.

Just as I did at IT Solutions, I worked every step of the Secret Sauce to earn the trust of the organization, cut costs, and increase sales, service contracts, and revenue. I'd like to share the following chart that shows a dramatic improvement in the financial results. It ranges between December 2003—which marked my first eight months on the job, mostly spent analyzing the situation and setting the Secret Sauce ingredients in motion—and December 2004, which marked my first full year as their transformational CEO in North America.

In the Appendix, pp. 186-189, you can find some cost charts, affectionately known as bullet trains, detailing just how focused this process was on costs such as telecons, freight, temporary employees, trade shows, corporate meetings, etc. As with so many other tools, I learned the bullet train concept at GE and applied it at all my other assignments. Just as the bullet train was created in Japan as a new concept to gain speed, we were looking for new conceptual thinking to quickly lower cost.

PHILIPS

SSR NA – December Key Financials

In million USD	December YTD		Variance
	2004	2003	
Order Intake	3,748.9	3,080.9	668.0
Sales	3,265.1	3,147.2	118.0
Gross Margin	897.8	811.4	86.4
% of Sales	27.5%	25.8%	1.7%
S,G&A/R&D Exp	(580.1)	(571.1)	(9.0)
% of Sales	-17.8%	-18.1%	0.4%
IFO adjusted	284.7	192.2	92.6
% of Sales	8.7%	6.1%	2.7%
Inventory	217.8	251.5	(33.7)
Cash Flow	373.0	275.0	98.0

Medical – December MBRM SSR N.A.   17

I believe you can readily read the story this chart tells, but I'd like
to briefly explain what these numbers meant to me. First, we increased
our orders by almost $700 million, which created a robust backlog/pipe-
line that assured our future success. We increased sales—actual product
installation or new service revenue—by $118 million and gross margin
on sales by $86 million, which both had a direct impact on earnings.
Margins went up because we were reducing or holding costs flat in a
growth environment and getting improved prices. We slightly decreased
our overhead expenses: sales, general and administrative, research and
development (S,G&A/R&D) on a percentage of sales basis, a remarkable achievement considering our growth.

IFO is an acronym for income from operations, the term Philips
used for earnings. So we increased earnings by $92.6 million—almost
50% higher than the previous year—and made earnings a significantly
higher percentage of sales. Put simply, we were delivering on all financial
fronts, which had not been happening for two years in North America.

Inventory decreased by more than $33 million, which meant we
were selling what we were taking from the manufacturers. Finally, cash
flow increased by almost $100 million. Cash is king, and a company

that has substantial cash reserves is much more likely to further invest in its future.

Looking at this chart today, I am proud of what we accomplished in a short time. Throughout this chapter, I have emphasized that you can't be a transformational leader unless you improve financial results, and I definitely accomplished that in my tenure of less than two years as CEO. I left Philips for USIS in early 2005, shortly after this chart was created, and the business was in much better financial shape than when I arrived. In the end, that's what being a transformational leader is all about: leaving behind a stronger team, a team that can perform without you, a team possessing a clear path forward to sustain its financial results.

US Investigations Services (USIS)

I have already shared much of the USIS story, so I will keep this short. The fundamental financial problem I faced when I arrived was this: The company's revenue had grown dramatically due to the increased security needs after 9/11, as well as a number of acquisitions; but the growth in earnings had not kept pace with the growth in revenue. At the time Welsh Carson purchased USIS in 2003, revenue growth was more than 20% per year, but earnings growth was lagging well behind revenue growth. In a nutshell, I was engaged to bring earnings growth in line with revenue growth, and the greater goal was to create higher earnings growth than revenue growth.

The following chart includes some key numbers from 2004, the year before I arrived at USIS, through 2008, my last year as CEO:

Year	Revenue	Earnings	% growth in Revenue	% growth in Earnings
2004	$500 M	$100 M	N/A	N/A
2005	$750 M	$108 M	50%	8%
2006	$781 M	$125 M	4%	15.7%
2007	$828 M	$140 M	6%	12%
2008	$881 M	$184 M	6.4%	31.4%

As you can see, even though revenue growth slowed somewhat for a number of reasons, we had significant value growth through the transformation of our earnings results. My team and I accomplished this by working all the Secret Sauce ingredients, transforming the organization's strategic thinking to focus on earnings as our true measure of success. As in all businesses, significant earnings growth was waiting to be realized. We just needed the right people, a much stronger cost focus, lots of technology application, improved metrics, and significant operating-process discipline to realize the above results.

I also worked hard to educate the employees. I showed them how earnings are the lifeblood of any business, and that a business where earnings don't keep pace with revenue is a business in decline. It cannot fulfill the goals of its investors and cannot invest in rewarding employees to the degree they need and expect to feel like winners. Our actions helped them to understand how growth in earnings allows a company to offer better compensation and benefits. They came to believe this as they saw their compensation and benefits improve with the business's success. This is critical to winning and maintaining employee loyalty. Your employees must share in the business's success!

Along with my mantra of People, Process, Productivity, and Growth, I emphasized the need for earnings growth again and again in my AskRandy messages. The previous leadership did a great job of growing revenue but lagged on earnings, and, as I have mentioned, they lacked clear numbers-oriented communication. Paul has told me that he felt the AskRandy messages for my first year at USIS were like a course in Business 101, and I would say that is true. You can't be a successful transformational leader unless your organization understands the details: where you are trying to take them, why that is the business direction they must obtain, and what is in it for them if they achieve these objectives.

Concluding Thoughts

From the three business stories I have relayed in this chapter, you can readily see that the Secret Sauce was the foundation and process for greatly improved financial results at three very different businesses. GE Capital IT Systems was a business in crisis, pure and simple. Philips was a business in denial...denial that the acquisitions were not adequately integrated, denial that there were too many leaders, and denial of inadequate financial results. I would call USIS a business in the shadows. Its employees had limited knowledge and no voice in the business, which caused it to have poor financial performance when better performance was just waiting in the shadows.

I used every tool and technique that I have shared with you in the previous six chapters to improve the financial results at these three different businesses. However, I want to emphasize that you just can't take the Secret Sauce and think you will be a transformational leader and a financial success. You have to know and understand your business, adapting the Sauce as necessary for the financial needs of your specific situation. I had to use the Sauce differently at each of these three businesses. For example, let's consider the tool where the Sauce begins: communication.

AT GE Capital IT Solutions, the business had been built by numerous acquisitions, so the employees for the most part understood little of the GE culture. I had to respect the fact they were not accustomed to this straightforward business culture: "I'll tell you like it is, tell you what we're going to do, and tell you when we're going to do it." I had to sell them on the fact that they came from disparate backgrounds, had been pulled together into one business, and it wasn't working for myriad reasons. I told them I didn't know the total solution, but I was going to use every tool I could to take cost out of the business and return it to profitability. It wasn't a pleasant message, but there was no other choice.

At Philips, in order to transform future financial results, I had to shift a stoic, slow-moving corporate culture into high speed and communicate that denying the need to integrate the acquisitions was no longer acceptable. I had to tell them, "Look folks, you're not going to like this, but here's the deal. I know I'm not at GE anymore and that you're used to a different way of doing business, but we're not going to get where we need to go unless we adopt some of the GE practices and attributes that I have learned." Then the first clear message I had to deliver was a tough one: "To create one Philips, we will need significantly less managers than we have today."

At USIS, I had to walk in and say, "Tell me what's wrong. Here's who I am, here's how I communicate, and here's what a vision looks like, but let me hear from you what the real problems are. I had to sell a whole new way of looking at the business and encourage communication from everyone in the organization—something they had never been allowed, let alone encouraged, to do.

The great reward of being a transformational leader who is successful at improving financial results is not just the salary, stock options, and other incentives, but the career opportunities that financial success creates. I was able to leave GE and move on to Philips because of the success I achieved at GE Capital IT Solutions and a host of other GE assignments. I entered the private equity world of USIS because of my success at Philips, coupled with my extensive GE background. I moved to my current job with the former owners of USIS, the private equity firm Welsh, Carson, Anderson & Stowe, because of my USIS success.

I am so excited by all I have learned about transformational leadership through my experiences, and I am even more excited to share the Secret Sauce with other leaders, would-be leaders, and those working to grow professionally. Transformational leadership is not easy. It requires hard work. You will make mistakes and have to start over again. Here's my suggestion:

If you have read and understand these seven chapters on the Secret Sauce of transformational leadership, but are unsure how to apply those lessons to your present situation, get some coaching. Get some mentoring. Ask Randy if you want. I would love to hear from you and help you apply the Secret Sauce to your unique situation. You can contact me at: rdobbs@pbros.net.

As I close this section of the book, let me remind you: There is a lifetime of learning, success, failures, and unfathomable experiences that developed my Secret Sauce. Good luck on creating your own Secret Sauce recipe!

MORE
VALUES

CHAPTER 11

Focus on the Customer or Spoil the Secret Sauce!

There's a joke about a guy in a very tough, competitive business environment, so tough and competitive he begins to close his business. As he's doing that, he finds a magic lamp, rubs it, and out pops a genie. "I will grant you one wish," says the genie, "but I must warn you that whatever you wish for, your competitor will receive double." The man thinks for a while, then smiles and says, "I want to be blind in one eye."

Even if your competition is blind—which is highly unlikely—your customers will never be blind to poor service, poor quality, or poor relationships. In the last chapter, I shared that driving financial results is the real end product of the Secret Sauce, but I contend that you can't sustain financial results unless you maintain and relentlessly grow customer satisfaction. If you taint your brand, your product, or reputation in your customers' eyes, your financial results will go down the drain along with the rest of all your work on the Sauce.

No business will grow without committed customers. To develop and maintain customers you have to continually work to build customer relationships. You have to know your customers' businesses, their needs, and their plans. You must get out of the office and see your customers.

The ultimate question to ask your customers is, "Would you recommend our business to someone you know?" Do you really know how your customers would answer that question? Do you know what it would take to get a positive answer for your business? Other questions could also be critical as you get to know your customers, such as, "Are you satisfied with your sales rep? How is our delivery performance? Do we follow up on your issues?"

These and other questions could help your organization receive a positive recommendation, but first and foremost you must ask your customers how they feel. It's good if you ask and your customer tells you what is wrong. It's business death if you don't listen and act.

The old saying is true: The customer is always right. The only exception is when a customer's demands are unreasonable relative to your desired financial performance, as I discussed regarding my experience at GE Capital IT Solutions—an unusual scenario. In most cases, the customer is not only always right, but also the driving force for your business. Your business only exists as long as your customers desire what you have to offer. The silent killer for a business is a dissatisfied customer, because most dissatisfied customers quit you quietly. Customer loyalty is achieved one transaction at a time.

When I worked at the GE Motors plant in Jonesboro, I naively believed our customers bought our motors because GE produced them. Really...as naïve as that sounds today, I was so focused on output that I did not think strongly enough about this fact: the GE monogram only signaled quality and customer sensitivity if we *delivered* that as a supplier.

Later, after my experience as a plant manager in Mexico, I took a job as manager of commercial marketing for GE Motors in Fort Wayne, Indiana. That's where I really came to understand that customers bought our products because our products satisfied their business needs, which in turn were driven by their own end-customers' needs. You can't just produce a product; you have to produce exactly the kind of product that satisfies your customers' total needs regarding price, performance, quality, design, etc. You might want to produce vanilla, and your sales team might want to sell chocolate; but if your customers want strawberry, that's what you'd better produce and sell if you want to stay in business.

The same is true in a service business. I have already shared the idea that both GE Medical Systems and Philips Medical Systems made a strategic shift from focusing on selling high-end medical equipment to selling equipment, service, and solutions. This shift was totally driven by our earnings objectives and changing customer requirements. The customers in this market had always been driven to purchase equipment fueled by technology advances, but, as conditions changed in most hospital financial situations, they needed options to stretch their capital funding other than just buying new technology. So this drove equipment leasing as an alternative to selling it, and service contracts to ensure new levels of equipment up-time expectations to serve more patients around the clock, generating additional revenue for the hospitals.

All of this supports the fact that customers buy for two reasons. Assuming your customer is not an end user, the customer buys because 1) you improve their ability to compete in their own business environment, and 2) because you make their business better and their job easier.

The dynamic is similar for an end user, but the situation is different. End users buy because 1) you improve their ability to compete or function in a challenging world, and 2) because you make their lives better or more productive. In both cases, it comes down to the fact that you **add value.**

I came to understand what it really means to add value in my first job outside of the Jonesboro plant—as a GE Motors national account manager for Whirlpool, one of our biggest customers and our staunchest competitor. I took this job after 10 years at the plant because Bill Fenoglio—who had become my sponsor in the GE organization—told me that I needed cross-functional experience in sales to reach my full potential as a leader. I needed stronger customer orientation.

At the time I took this job, I had risen through the ranks to become manager of shop operations, just one step down from the plant manager. So I was moving from a factory, where more than 800 people counted on my hourly decisions, to the role of an individual contributor in a position where I had no experience prior to the assignment. This turned out to be a humbling yet invaluable experience. It started with a wild, all-day drive to South Bend, Indiana, just after Christmas, with my wife, myself, and our two children all suffering from stomach flu. We had to stop every two hours to throw up behind the U-Haul. What a way to make my first family and career move in GE!

The job situation was worse than the move. I reported to a district manager who was frustrated, stuck with a guy with no sales experience but anointed by the big boss. A significant part of his evaluation process was a point system. It didn't focus much on sales, but rather on relationships and the number of times I took a customer to lunch, dinner, a play, a sporting event, or other activities.

Every week I hit the road, making the rounds of the Whirlpool Corporate HQ in Benton Harbor, Michigan, three Whirlpool plants in

Ohio, and a parts distribution center in LaPorte, Indiana. Whirlpool no longer bought motors from us, but they did buy range timers, capacitors, and other components. They bought as few as they could because we were the enemy as an appliance end-product competitor. Now I was the enemy sales rep, with little experience, a family unhappy about moving to the North in the dead of winter, and an inner heartache for my former operations leadership role.

On top of all that, my primary relationship was with a corporate buyer who looked at me as nothing more than a source of lunches with three silver bullets—vodka on the rocks—and boxes of his favorite golf balls. At the plants, I made some appropriate contacts, but I spent weeks working to see plant managers to put relationship points on the board with guys who wouldn't see just another sales guy.

Finally, I realized I should use my experience in plant operations to my advantage. So I worked to create the opportunity to share my background with one plant manager's secretary and told her I had some good ideas from my plant observations that could improve their operation. She suggested I write a note to the manager. To my great surprise, on my next visit he scheduled a 45-minute lunch meeting that turned into two hours!

By the time I reached the next plant late that afternoon, there was a note that the plant manager wanted to spend some time with me. Suddenly the doors were open at the Whirlpool plants, because they discovered that I was capable of doing more than sell; I was willing to add value by offering my experience in plant operations to help them with their own operations.

Although I took a different approach, I played within the district manager's system, treating my new contacts to meals and events, and became one of the top-ranked salesmen in my district as measured by his point system. An interesting side note: While I disdained his point system and all the social events, his emphasis on relationships pushed me to my actions with the plant managers. Relationships do count!

More important, I increased sales in a hostile market and learned an invaluable lesson: **Customers buy because we sell to them—not because we have products or services to offer—and the most powerful way to sell is to convince the customer that you can bring something to that transaction that adds value to their business or their life.**

The only way to really know what will add value to a customer's business or life is to develop a relationship with the customer. Obviously, some businesses have too many customers to develop direct relationships with all of them, but they use marketing tools such as focus groups, surveys, and industry organizations to gain as clear a picture as possible of their customers and their needs. This is the single biggest customer-related "miss" that businesses make...not getting to know your customers to the point where they will tell you what they need.

How do you develop relationships? At the risk of sounding like a broken record, I will say it again: You have to get out of the office and visit customers. Where a leader spends his or her time drives the business results you get both internally and externally. You have to connect with the customer on the level that will best facilitate real, honest feedback on delivery, cost, quality, sales effectiveness, and how they rate you vs. your competition.

Every situation is different. In my sales job, I realized that the plant managers wanted to improve their plants, and I had the experience to help them do it. At Philips and GE Medical Systems, our customers were radiologists, cardiologists, and other high-level medical professionals with big egos and huge responsibilities. I had to understand and play to that in order to establish a relationship. At USIS, our customers for federal background investigations were under pressure from the Administration and Congress to improve cycle times on investigations. I had to profusely and sincerely apologize for our shortcomings and work with them to meet the federal requirements placed on them.

One of my most interesting exercises in customer relations was at the GE Motors plant in Reynosa, Mexico. Our customers had some fear and uncertainty about buying products manufactured in Mexico. So we invited our customers to visit the plant, where young employees and teams, with a team leader capable of speaking good English, gave them a tour. It worked wonders. They not only saw the plant operation, in many ways better than plant operations in the United States, but also got to know some of our best employees. They began to feel comfortable with the idea that we were achieving success within the Mexican culture.

Getting to know your customer's needs and adding value remain the bottom line to successful customer relations, but there are three other drivers: price, quality, and convenience.

Think about the dry cleaning business. It seems like there's a dry cleaner on almost every corner in most cities, so how do you decide which dry cleaner to patronize? Most people will either pick the closest one or will follow a friend's recommendation. The next question: What would make you change dry cleaners? Typically, the answer is determined by unreasonable price or poor quality much more than convenience. Most of us would not make a longer trip unless price or quality is significantly objectionable.

You will seldom go to another dry cleaner, even if you discover it does the same quality work for a better price; but you're unlikely to stick with the convenient cleaner if its quality does not meet your expectations. Conversely, you might go to a more expensive cleaner if you believe it will provide higher quality. Price, quality, and convenience work together in a customer's mind. The customer will buy from the business that offers the combination that meets the customer's needs.

Beyond these drivers, there is still the relationship you build with your customer. No one goes to a dry cleaner for companionship, but if the person behind the counter is rude or indifferent, you're much more likely to change than if he or she were friendly, professional, and personable—despite price or convenience. However, poor quality work on your clothes will be the killer of even a great business personality.

You may provide your customer with convenience, price, quality, or all three; but you will never achieve your full potential with your customers unless you get to know them and really understand where needs rank in importance to them. In the end, your customer's perception of your business is the reality! That reality will fill the sails of your business's ship or will likely sink your enterprise.

CHAPTER 12

Be Proud of Your Heritage and What Defines You

Professor John Imhoff, former head of the University of Arkansas's Department of Industrial Engineering, came up with a theory now known as Imhoff's Law: "The organization of any bureaucracy is very much like a septic tank—the really big chunks always rise to the top."

I hope that as we near this book's conclusion, you know enough about me to understand that I've never been and never wanted to be a big chunk. I'm sure some of my employees viewed me as a big chunk, but that's not how I see myself. I think it goes back to my home environment, where I was just trying to survive. I distinguished myself as a performer early on in school and in sports, but I had a lot more angst about who I was than bravado about my accomplishments. My grandmother was a successful person, but she didn't raise me to think I was better than anyone else. She taught me to say "please" if I wanted something and "thank you" if I got it. She taught me to say, "Yes, sir; No, sir; Yes, ma'am; No, ma'am."

These are traditional Southern values, and fundamentally they define who I am: a Southerner. In fact, I was so steeped in being a Southerner growing up that I didn't even know I had a Southern accent until we moved north to Springfield, Illinois, where my father got a job selling chemicals. On our first night there, we went out to dinner at McDonald's. We didn't do that often, and his rule was that we could have a cheeseburger, fries, and a coke—but if we wanted a milkshake, we had to skip the fries, because the milkshake was more expensive than a coke. Now, I loved chocolate milkshakes and I loved fries, so this was a quandary for me. On this particular night, however, my father said we could have anything we wanted—his way of helping us adjust to the move.

I was old enough to order for myself, so I stepped up to the counter and said, "Ah wahnt a chawcolate milkshake, some friiies, and a cheeeeeseburger." The girl behind the counter just looked at me and laughed out loud. "Son," she said. "If you say that again, I'll give it to you for free."

Everyone talked like that back in Auburn, so I never knew there was any other way of speaking. Now I was in Yankee country, and I guess I sounded pretty funny. I was a little embarrassed, but I said it again, and sure enough she gave me the meal for free.

I don't have as heavy a Southern accent today, but I still have a noticeable accent, and I'm never going to stop having that accent. It's part of who I am and where I'm from, and I'm proud of it, just as my grandmother was.

I can tell you from experience that there's a certain prejudice in the business world toward Southerners. My Southern accent was no big deal when I began my GE career at the plant in Jonesboro, Arkansas; but as I moved up in the GE ranks, I faced a lot of mockery and teasing. Some of it was funny, but a lot of it was mean-spirited. I was definitely looked down upon because of my accent and my state college education, but it never stopped me from getting where I wanted to go. I never tried to change the way I spoke and never hesitated to speak publicly; in fact, public speaking is one of my greatest strengths. The audience just has to get used to the fact that I might say, "Cheeeeeseburger."

Like most defining traits, my Southern heritage and humble roots are both a weakness that I had to work through and a strength that makes me the leader I am today. Sometimes at GE I felt like such an outsider that I believe I got a taste of what it feels like to be a minority—not a pleasant feeling. However, by working through others' prejudice and embracing who I am, I became a stronger person and a better leader. I never changed my core values that built the Secret Sauce described in this book.

Another experience that defined me as a person was my one year teaching sixth grade before I began my business career. I absolutely loved teaching, and that year made me a teacher/coach for life. In Chapter 7, Karen Query praised my mentoring skills—which I really appreciate, because mentoring is something of a crusade for me. Some of my most satisfying experiences in the business world have been helping a struggling employee to succeed.

However, it's also been a weakness I've had to work through. As I shared in chapter 7, when I started out in the business world, I wanted to save everyone, just as I wanted all of my sixth graders to make it to the seventh grade. You can do that in the classroom, but you just can't save everyone in the business world, especially as you move up into leadership positions. That's because the actions of others become the most critical element of your own success.

I learned to accept that I couldn't get everyone to seventh grade in the business world, but I never liked it and still don't. The combination of my background and my teaching experience gave me a lot of empathy for other people, and I have suffered inside every time I've had to let people go. I shared the experience at GE Capital IT Solutions (ITS) and how I hated the big turnaround task, knowing I had to fire people, and lots of them. Unfortunately, that wasn't my first experience of mass firing.

Earlier in my career, I rose to become manager of shop operations at the Jonesboro plant. Whirlpool, a major customer, decided that they would no longer buy motors from GE because we were a competitor in manufacturing appliances. Overnight, we lost almost a third of our business. I had to lay off more than a third of the workforce, hundreds of employees. These weren't people I had just met or never met, like the employees at ITS. These were people in my hometown, people I had worked with for years, people I knew and cared about. It was a painful experience, but I understood that it had to be done, and I did it while maintaining production for our remaining customers and continuing to improve plant productivity.

Just as important, I believe I did it in as sensitive and humane a way as I could. If the inner pain is the bad side of having empathy, the good side is this: I have always treated people the way I would like to be treated. In the end, that has not only generated respect from others but also provided peace of mind during the task.

From these few examples, you can see how remaining true to yourself in a competitive environment can be a double-edged sword. Often the greatest strengths that help you grow are also weaknesses you have to grow around. I don't believe you have to change who you are, but if who you are is getting in the way of your success, you have to change how you *act*. For example, as I just discussed, I hated firing people but I did it anyway, because there was no other way for the businesses to survive. I didn't change my identity as a Southerner, but I did work on becoming more polished in a high-level business setting. I never lost my desire to save everyone, but I did learn to discipline myself and do what was best for the business.

If you feel your weaknesses are holding you back, I can offer two suggestions:

1. **Get a professional coach.** Look within your business and establish a relationship with someone more experienced, or whose approach to the business environment you admire. Some companies have formal mentoring programs in which senior leaders tutor up-and-coming leaders. GE has a long history of very successful mentoring programs, and we established a mentoring program at USIS that remains a big success.

   You might also find a mentor outside your business, maybe a friend or acquaintance. The key is to find someone who will make an effort to understand who you are and give you honest, objective feedback and practical suggestions on how to turn your weaknesses into strengths.

2. **Surround yourself with people whose strengths compliment your weaknesses.** When I came to USIS, I hired a CFO named Dave Kaminsky, with whom I had worked at GE ITS. Dave is a wizard at the financial aspects of running a business, and he knew the GE way. He had been tested like myself in several other tough GE Capital business assignments. When I arrived, we had an excellent CFO, Phil Sweeney, whom I mentioned in Chapter 7 as the only real "keeper" among my senior leaders. It was important to keep Phil in the business, but he was getting a little tired of the daily grind of being the CFO and was ready to move into another position as senior vice president for corporate development. Phil used his finance background very effectively, identifying several strategic acquisitions, helping us to win a notable acquisition, and significantly impacting the business's success. Dave built a strong financial team. He also taught me a lot along the way—how to more effectively change our business and communicate our financial objectives to the staff. We were a great team, and the power of two people who compliment each other is always stronger than the power of one.

✳ ✳ ✳ ✳

The business world can be a tough environment, and the further you progress in your career, the tougher the challenges become. I have given you the Secret Sauce as a way to meet those challenges and transform your organization. However, while you are transforming your organization, be watchful that you do not lose yourself. Growth is imperative for all of us, but we do not have to change who we are in order to grow; in fact, we grow better and stronger by understanding our heritage and the experiences and character traits that define us.

I'd like to close this chapter with my own version of a famous quote from Shakespeare: "To thine own self be true." My version is, "To thine own self be true...but build a strong, differentiated team." People will always differ in values, needs, skills, and preferences. Despite who you are, don't try to oversell your values, skills, and experience. Try to find common ground to create a sense of purpose that allows you to focus on common needs, so all of the varied skills and values can work together to optimize the results.

On page 192 of the Appendix, you will find a Randy Dobbs 4-block chart, which always helps me to reflect on who I am, what I've learned, and where I can go from here. It's a helpful exercise, and I urge you to try it for yourself.

CHAPTER 13

One Team or No Team...
There's No Choice

To me, one of the greatest team stories ever is the 1980 U.S. Olympic hockey team. Just two weeks after being trounced 10-3 by the world-champion Soviets in a pre-Olympic match-up, a young but gritty U.S. team completely committed to each other, coming back to defeat not only the Soviets but also powerful teams from Sweden, Czechoslovakia, and Finland. They won the gold medal at the Lake Placid Olympics, a team feat that is still marveled at today. Teams truly can accomplish what individuals often don't believe is possible.

I've shared the story of how, when I joined Philips Medical Systems North America, I found five separate teams, including the original Philips personnel and others from the four recent acquisitions. I worked through many ideas and initiatives at Philips, but my single-most important action was to integrate those five teams into one team. Like the Olympic hockey team, they could only accomplish market greatness with a common cause and structure.

The same was true at GE Capital ITS, which consisted of more than 40 global acquisitions. There were really no true team processes, metrics, structure, or identity when I arrived, and most of the employees had even less knowledge of the GE way. There will be no real greatness or true optimization of accomplishments in any group without first establishing the concept, structure, and ground rules for team play.

Philips and ITS were unusual situations, but in order to transform any business there is no more fundamental change than the molding into one team. In sports we use the word "team" to describe a group of players who compete together against their opponents, but there are different kinds of teams. In fact, some teams aren't teams at all; they're just individuals who are playing together. We hear about teams with "problems in the locker room," and they often don't perform up to their potential. On the other hand, teams that have a great locker-room atmosphere may not perform at a level equal to or beyond their potential due to lack of leadership. However, if you can create a cohesive team of individuals willing to work as a team and provide them the right leader, I contend that team can accomplish amazing things!

It's exactly the same in the business world. The business team must have a "locker room unity," which means commitment to each other behind the scenes as well as in the trenches, and leadership they can respect and believe in day-to-day to drive the team concept.

The movement to one team must be accompanied by movement of power, knowledge, and rewards to all levels of the business. Today in the USIS investigations business, the team leaders, who are four levels below USIS CEO Bill Mixon, know fundamentally as much about the business's performance and metrics as the upper levels of field management. They know that their performance assessments and performance rewards are based on that knowledge and ownership. In many respects, the team leaders have as much or more capability and potential than the senior leaders to drive and transform business success. When I arrived in 2005, the divisional president ran the ISD business with a very top-down approach. Today, there are 200 potential Bill Mixons—the team leaders—running the business from the bottom up.

As I have mentioned, I am no longer involved with USIS, but Paul is, and he shared an interesting example with me. As I write this, USIS is giving most of its investigators a substantial and much-deserved pay raise to sustain the company's market competitiveness. The team leaders are reviewing the pay raise with every single investigator, whether or not he or she received the raise, and explaining the basis for the raise decision. This is ownership at the lowest leadership level, and it demonstrates how the team leaders own the team and its performance. It also forces every investigator to commit as an integral part of the team and the performance results of a 15-17-member team vs. the broader team of 3,000 investigators.

This "everyone is on the team" approach changes what people are expected to do every day. It changes what being a part of the business means to them. When people think for themselves, when they manage their work and time, when they take responsibility for customer satisfaction, when they accept other responsibilities and accountability, they move from just showing up for work to actually owning the business at their level.

As a transformational leader, you have to create a conducive environment, setting expectations that **every employee will "bring his or her brain to work" every day.** To succeed in a competitive business world, you need every brain engaged, thinking about cost, customer satisfaction, and how to build and sustain the business's future. In an organization of 7,000 people, this is impossible to accomplish without team metrics, team leadership, team rewards, and team accountability.

As you are moving toward this one-team solution, everyone in the organization will—as I'm sure you've heard before—either be part of the solution or part of the problem. This transformation will never be trouble-free. There will always be people who either don't understand what a team really means or just don't want to accept the team process. Every employee must either get "on or off the team train." You as the leader must make it clear without a doubt that, if they don't join the team train, they will be left at the proverbial station. The business will move on without them. This is a tough but simple stance you must take, with no exceptions, no loners, if you really want to build a team.

Problems are the price of progress, and I'll share a good example of this from USIS. When I arrived, the investigators drove their own cars, and we had no way to control costs and feared our uncontrolled insurance liability. The menagerie of vehicles impacted our professional image, causing concern for the safety of our investigators, as we had no way of knowing the condition of their vehicles.

Faced with this situation, we decided to shift to a company-car program for our field staff. Most investigators received a brand new car and a gas card, and we paid all insurance and maintenance costs. They were allowed unlimited personal use of the car for a very reasonable monthly Personal Use Charge.

We thought this was a win-win program for employees and for the company, but the amount of resistance was amazing. Some people always resist change, and in this case, I believe many of the investigators did not fully understand the program. Ultimately, we implemented this program successfully by having the team leaders own the education and implementation at the local level. We allowed the changes to be implemented on timing that worked for the local team, relevant to concerns or vehicle commitments such as leases or extended car payments on personal vehicles.

This example also demonstrates another critical facet of building one team. Once the team process gains momentum, allowing real decision-making power, the team often progresses faster than some of the team's individuals. When that happens, the unique process of resistance by a few will usually yield one of two results: either those resistant individuals will join the team in change, or the team will not allow them to remain in the process with unreasonable resistance. The power of the team can often accomplish things that would take much longer to achieve with management mandates!

Teaming is a never-ending task. They're still building teams at USIS, as they are at every business I have touched as a transformational leader. This goes back to my chart on a manager vs. a leader. Managers usually establish a one-team process in which they control the team to their benefit and desires. Leaders, who build teams with few mandates, know that teams only progress if they are allowed to experiment and grow at varied rates, just as a family grows and changes over time.

True leadership is all about empowerment, accountability, and change, and that is what continually drives the team process. Throughout my career, most of the best ideas came from people on the teams who were working in the trenches, living in the middle of day-to-day issues. They see the issues and often see solutions, but they will only develop and communicate these solutions if they feel empowered to do so.

I'll say it again: You want every brain engaged, as the power of thousands of brains in growing and improving your business can prove truly remarkable. The leader holds the key to unlocking the power of this team process.

During my Reynosa experience, we empowered teenagers, often with only eighth-grade educations, to form various operational teams. As I've shared in a previous chapter, we then found an individual on each team who spoke English, making him or her responsible for customer tours so our American customers would buy into the concept of buying products manufactured in Mexico. The combination of the teams and the tours gave the kids a real sense of ownership and empowerment. This significantly improved turnover, quality, and output, not to mention how much it progressed our relationships with manufacturers using our product in the United States.

At GE Capital ITS, employee task forces drove many of the changes and cost take-outs, eliminating thousands of jobs and communicating to leadership how to consolidate our operations while maintaining customer relations. I knew what I had to do with that business in a general sense; but *the teams* told me the best ways to accomplish and survive the major business overhaul.

Team momentum, not the CEO, drives a business's future. Once you establish that momentum, the business and the teams will continue to grow as the teams go forward. You can't destroy team momentum without destroying the business.

Why is it essential to change to a one-team, participative organization? There are many benefits, and I have shared some of them in this chapter. However, I believe there is one answer more important than any other: Not only a business's survival, but its future and all its current and future jobs, depend on this team approach. Teaming is not just an exercise, nor should it be viewed as a business fad. It is the *only* way to make everyone in the organization accountable for your enterprise's future success.

Unifying one team is hard work, but it is the most rewarding accomplishment of my long business career. I can still see the impact I made by creating one team in the organizations I have led, and the impact those teams are continuing to make. The team will keep on changing, but once you create a one-team mentality, the organization will never retreat from that mentality; in fact, the organization will no longer accept team members who don't care or choose not to be a part of the team.

I will end this chapter with a quote I love about the importance of a fully committed team. In 1966, UCLA surprised the entire football world by upsetting Michigan State—a team at that time thought to be the greatest college football team ever—by a score of 14-12 in the Rose Bowl. After the game, Coach Tommy Prothro of UCLA said, "If one person on this team had put out just one percent less, we would have lost."

It is much the same in the business world. The difference between a great business and an average business is, in most instances, the majority of the people's engagement in that business working together and optimizing the business's results as a team—not the results of various individuals. The stronger the team, the more team players who give 100%, the greater the potential for success!

CHAPTER 14
It's Never Too Late to Change

Early in this book, I shared how my grandmother left my grandfather in California during the depths of the Great Depression, returning to Auburn, Alabama, to care for her widowed mother and help run the family business. That story illustrates the impressive courage it takes to change, especially for a woman of her era, fighting many challenges and societal taboos, to make such a dramatic life transformation.

The story's happy ending demonstrates the truth of this chapter's title: "It's Never Too Late to Change." I was about twelve years old when my grandmother made a decision to change in the 1960s that amazes me still more than her courageous change in the 1930s. She and my grandfather had been divorced for almost 30 years. He had remarried and established a successful life as a lawyer in California. Suddenly he was diagnosed with leukemia, and his second wife decided she could not deal with his imminent death. He located and contacted my grandmother, then followed up with a cross-county trip to Auburn. He told her he had maybe two years to live and that that he had always loved her. He asked if she would consider dating again, now that his second wife had left him. More important, he asked if she would do it out of love, not pity.

My grandmother had remained single, devoting her life to family and work. She told my grandfather that she wouldn't date him, but she would marry him again and enjoy their time together until he died. She said that leaving him was the biggest mistake she'd ever made. If he wanted to live in California, that was fine with her. She'd move to California and follow him wherever he wanted to go—and that's exactly what she did. She left the laundry and the big, white house with her brother and his children, and packed up herself and her mother, forsaking the place they loved, to live with my grandfather in California. She was almost 60 years old, but she wasn't afraid to make a dramatic change. As it turned out, my grandfather outlived the disease's prognosis, and they enjoyed almost 10 more years together.

I talked with my grandmother about this in later years, after my grandfather died. She confided that she had been a successful businesswoman but had neglected the feelings of her heart. She genuinely loved my grandfather, and he loved her. So she totally reversed her path, while staying true to herself.

My grandfather may have been dying, but he was a bright guy who made money as a lawyer, an insurance salesman, and buying and selling real estate. For the first time in 30 years, my grandmother didn't have to worry about earning a living. I visited them often in California, and they were quite a pair! They traveled to Mexico and moved several times in California. I think it's pretty romantic that these two dynamic people, who shared their closing years with a zest for life together, got a second chance at romance.

When I made my decision to leave GE and take the CEO job at Philips Medical Systems North America, I thought about my grandmother and how brave she was to change late in life. I was 52 and had been a GE guy for 28 years. I never imagined working for another company, but it was clear to me that the new GE leadership did not want for me the future I wanted at GE. So I moved across the country alone, from Atlanta to Seattle—a place where I knew no one—and began a brand new chapter of my life and career.

As you know from reading the previous chapters, the Philips job turned out to be a wonderful opportunity. It spring-boarded me to a true business CEO role at USIS, and ultimately to the very fulfilling job I have today in the private-equity world. Although I give full credit to GE for the education and experiences forming the core of my transformational leadership, I have become so much more because I had the courage to leave the GE cocoon and fly, even as an aging eagle. Like my grandmother, I was not afraid to change late in life and apply all I had learned to make those changes successful.

It's often said that the only constant in the universe is change, and I strongly believe that is true. No matter what age you are, change is inevitable, but people react to change in different ways. How do you react? How will you react to the changes you will face now and for the rest of your life?

These are questions only you can answer, but I'd like to offer an example to consider. I was on the beach last summer, watching a series of good-sized waves roll in toward shore. The people in the water reacted to these waves in three different ways, and it struck me that their reactions formed a good metaphor for the way people react to change.

Some people dove into and under each wave. They held their breath as the wave washed over them, pinning them to the bottom until the turbulence had passed. Then they popped back up again in exactly the same place, and faced the next wave rolling in.

Other people turned their bodies at an angle to each oncoming wave and jumped as high as they could to keep their heads above the water. The force of the wave hit them hard, stinging and slapping against them. When the wave had passed, they too were in about the same spot, facing the next wave.

Still others waited bravely until the wave was about to break. They pushed off and swam as hard as they could, just ahead of the break, until the wave caught them in its force, carrying them on an exhilarating ride all the way into shore. These people emerged smiling and laughing, then swam back out to catch the next wave.

In ocean swimming, no one can catch every wave, and there are times when it is appropriate to dive under or jump above it. In the business world, it's ALWAYS better to catch the wave and ride with it. It's even better if you can anticipate the break and swim just ahead, so you're ready when it comes. If you do that, you'll be the one moving while others are standing still. And if you build one team and the team catches the wave together, you can accomplish anything.

Change has eternal life. You may dive under the wave and stay in much the same place, but really you are always going forward or going backward, because—if others are catching the wave and you are standing still—you are falling behind. This is true of a leader, an employee, a parent, a spouse, a student—whatever you do, you have to catch the wave's leading edge.

The waves keep rolling in and the winds of change keep blowing. Think of our nation: As I write this in late 2009, the winds of change have blown harder than in many years—maybe as hard as ever before. The economy, the military, healthcare, the administration, state and local governments, families, and individuals all face challenges that require change. Although it may seem that change lies before us today with a special urgency, the fact is that change is always with us.

As a transformational leader, you must accept that change is a constant. You must live it, love it, and lead it. The great challenge of a transformational leader is this: How do you convince others to change?

Despite my humble background and education, I have always believed I have a gift for communication and persuasion. To use the old cliché, I believe I could sell ice to Eskimos. Throughout my career, I wasn't selling ice, of course—I was selling change...in every job and every situation. I am good at selling change, but it is never easy. To sell change you must make it personal. Those you are asking to change must believe in you, and, more important, you must win their trust that your actions are really going to improve their future odds of success.

People resist change and defend their old ways because they fear losing control. You must convince them that they can change while remaining in control, and, even better, convince them that they can control change by embracing it.

In the big picture, this book is all about my actions to drive transformational change, and they can be your actions, too. You must be open to change, and the tools in this book demonstrate how to change yourself and your organization. Even when you're using these tools, you have to keep questioning yourself, asking, "Am I doing this in the best interests of all involved? Am I really driving change that will last?"

I have done this all my life, and I never take for granted that change will be well understood, easy to do, or readily accepted. Real change is about winning people over on an ongoing basis, not some big, showy, one-time event.

In late 2006, my second year at USIS, I knew that our owners at Welsh Carson were preparing to market the company, and I faced tremendous pressure to drive performance. I was the only one who knew the company was going to be sold. We had recently lost our HR leader, so I searched for a new one and, as I mentioned in chapter 6, hired a very experienced leader named Dave Whitmore.

After Dave did his initial fact-finding, he told me that some of my new leaders did not feel comfortable with me and my leadership style. So we conducted another New Manager Assimilation exercise, responding to some still-unspoken concerns I believe stemmed from the pressure of the impending sale process that only I knew about. We had some new leaders by that time, and other leaders who had worked through the first New Manager Assimilation exercise were still uncomfortable with me. What I discovered from this exercise was enlightening and a little surprising. Here are some of the key issues:

- I had to improve my listening skills.

- I needed to focus on employee strengths rather than their weaknesses.

- I was spending too much time with the CFO and not enough time with other leaders.

- My patience and tolerance were not as good as they once had been.

- I was pushing too hard.

- I was setting stretch goals but not helping with the solutions.

These are sobering realizations for a transformational leader, but I accepted them as the truth. I knew I had to address these concerns to position the business for the return that Welsh Carson wanted and expected from the sale process. So, as I have done throughout my career, I listened to the feedback and modified my leadership approach. This helped achieve the results that enabled Welch Carson to sell the company at a good exit price, rewarding them, myself, and the senior leadership team.

As I believe you now know, I am a self-confident, accomplished transformational leader, but throughout my career I have never for a moment thought that I was above change or had all the answers. I have continually pushed myself to change in order to be a better leader. Even then it has not been enough, as I shared with you in this last example from late 2006.

It's never too late to listen, to adjust, to change your course. I contend that, if you desire to be a transformational leader, you **must** embrace this attitude of always improving—and I believe this is my first absolute "must" in the entire book.

Up to this point I have avoided discussing my favorite pastime: golf.

Those of you who also enjoy the punishment of this great sport can identify with the constant need to be willing to change to improve. Week to week, month to month, year to year, change is rewarded by the need for further change in order to master something you'll never master. That is what I meant by my first "must."

In closing, remember that change is not easy, but it's never too late to change and drive improvement in all aspects of your life.

Conclusion

Thanks for reading my first attempt to share my blueprint for transformational change outside the boundaries of any business I have led. I would be extremely disappointed if, in this book, I have not given you at least a couple of useful business-improvement ideas/tools.

Napoleon Bonaparte characterized leaders as "dealers in hope." Like all strong leaders, Napoleon knew that, for his organization, hope was the greatest of all possessions. I believe you can see from my real-life business examples that we gave some struggling business situations real transformational hope, which, when executed as described, moved from hope to transformational success.

I love to communicate, and some would say my love for this is ad nauseum. However, greater than my love for communication is my love for seeing others energized by their work, attracted to being a contributing part of an organization.

The antithesis of this is my biggest disappointment...to see good people, through no fault of their own, worry about their work future, fear their boss, and simply show up each day. Fundamentally, this situation results from a leader lacking the character to create an environment that facilitates passion for success in both work and life.

My credit for these thoughts goes to a multitude of experiences, but none greater than the experience and education I received at the GE Company. While I was finishing this book, I sent an email to Jack Welch, asking for a comment we could use on the cover. Although I did not know it, Jack was in the hospital at the time. He still replied to me within 48 hours, saying that he received so many requests for endorsements that he could not do it, but he was very proud of what I had accomplished in my career. He also wished me the best with what seemed to him to be an exciting book.

While I would have loved to have Jack's comment, what really matters is the kind of leader Jack was during his time at GE. My admiration for the transformational leadership I saw Jack drive in the GE Company is the real model and educational background for my success. Thanks, Jack...and thanks to all my readers!

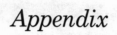

Appendix

AskRandy #1

US Investigations
services

TO: All USIS Employees

FROM: Randy Dobbs

AskRandy	Number 1	March 18, 2005

It is with great pleasure and enthusiasm that I join USIS as CEO at this exciting time in the company's development. Though I have only been part of the USIS community for fifteen days now, I appreciate the warm welcome I have received and am impressed by the high level of demonstrated commitment to our success. You are all responsible for this success, but I want to offer a special thanks to Phil Harper and his executive team. Their pioneering efforts have established a solid groundwork for the dynamic growth opportunities ahead.

As we move forward together, I will report to all USIS employees every other Friday in a letter addressing our successes, opportunities, and challenges. I ask that each and every one of you reference these messages in your daily work and strategic planning. By doing this, we will collectively continue to build momentum that will enable us to mature and develop our position as a premier supplier of security services.

I call these letters "AskRandy," because I want you to know that I am here to answer important questions you may have about our company, its present, and its future. I encourage you to contact me with these questions by email at AskRandy@usis.com. Since not everyone has access to email at this time, we are in the process of setting up a voicemail number. For now, let's begin with what is probably uppermost in your mind: Who am I, why was I selected for this position, and what does my selection mean to you and the USIS team?

What Is My Business Experience?

Over twenty-five years ago, I joined GE as a Process Control Specialist with the Specialty Motor Division—a particularly good fit since I had put myself through Arkansas State University working as an Apprenticed Machinist. I continually developed my career at GE by working in a number of positions in this division until I became a Field Sales Engineer with Component Sales. In 1984, I was promoted to Plant Manager of the GE Mexican affiliate. Four years later, I moved back to the U.S. as Manager of Commercial Marketing. I then moved over to GE Medical Systems, where I served as a Regional Manager for seven years. Changing businesses again, I became President and CEO of GE Capital IT Solutions of North America. Most recently, I served as President and CEO of Philips Medical Systems, North America, where I had responsibility for a $3.5 billion business with 5,500 employees spread across the U.S. and Canada.

How Do I View Myself?

On the positive side:

- I know that anything is possible if you want it badly enough.
- I am quick, decisive, and confident, and provide clear, direct leadership.
- I judge others by their ability to think and act quickly.
- I believe in a simple work structure: "Tell us what you are going to do, and do it."

On the other hand:

- I can be very impatient at times, driven by the will to win.
- I am often very candid, sometimes blunt, in order to speed up the process and clarify interpersonal communications.

What Do I Expect of You?

- Have character and integrity with the intention of always doing the right thing.
- Know where you are going and have a goal every day.
- Plan for the best but be prepared for things to go wrong—and have a backup plan.
- Communicate.
- Deliver results.
- Be flexible, have a tolerance for ambiguity, and be open to change.
- See yourself as part of something greater—a team.

What Will I Do in My First 90 Days?

- Spend time with every group of the team.
- Develop a common vision and energize the team.
- Review our organizational structure and address issues and opportunities.
- Establish clear and concise goals for 2005 and a plan to exceed them.
- Meet key customers.
- Develop a strategy to focus on successfully managing growth, both on the top line (sales) and the bottom line (operating income).

I am looking forward to getting to know the entire USIS team and hope that these biweekly emails will help us build and sustain a momentum of positive energy and successive wins as we move forward together.

Randy E. Dobbs
CEO

AskRandy #24

Number 24   **March 3, 2006**

TO: All USIS Employees

FROM: Randy Dobbs

As I write this message, my excitement continues to grow regarding the future of USIS. This week marks my one-year anniversary as your CEO, an appropriate time to look toward the future while considering the past. Even more exciting to me, however, are the first-ever USIS strategic planning sessions that we held in the Minneapolis-St. Paul area last week. In this AskRandy message, I'd like to share my thoughts on this first year and these first strategy sessions.

When I reflect on the journey we've taken together during the last year, I continue to be pleased by all we've accomplished. I have discussed many of those accomplishments in previous messages, but I would like to share with you what I consider to be the three most important total-business accomplishments: 1) we have strengthened leadership throughout the organization; 2) we are on a firmer financial footing, which will facilitate future growth; and 3) we are establishing a stronger, clearer, and more comprehensive USIS identity in the marketplace.

It's satisfying to take a moment to celebrate a milestone like this, but I am also very aware that the completion of one year means the beginning of another. I look forward with enthusiasm and optimism to the challenges and opportunities that lie ahead. We still have more to do, but we have a great team that will take us where we need to go. The strategic planning sessions gave me an opportunity to see our top leaders and their direct reports focused not only on performance but on great ideas to strategically grow the company in the future. I was very impressed by the quality of our leadership teams.

A Victory for One Is a Victory for All

At the start of the sessions, we received news that we won a significant recompete contract in PSD for the Iraqi National Police Development Division (NPDD). This means that we will continue our training presence there for another year with the possibility of two additional option years. The PSD team has been running this program for the past 20 months, providing the necessary infrastructure, training programs, and command and control support to develop a self-sustaining Iraqi internal security force. We have already helped Iraq field more than 3,800 security professionals, an important step toward a seamless and complete transition of the Iraqi NPDD from the U.S. government to the Iraqi Ministry of Interior. This is a nation-building project and a valuable contribution to the overall U.S. mission in Iraq.

Winning the recompete not only demonstrates the quality of the work we are doing in Iraq but also the strength and quality of the PSD team that worked so hard to win this important contract. Even though we were clearly the best and most experienced provider, there was tough competition, and the PSD team did everything possible and necessary to assure that we would emerge victorious.

When we announced the recompete win to the full group at the planning sessions, the room erupted in spontaneous applause. Every leader from the other businesses and corporate HQ shared the PSD team's sense of excitement and success. They viewed the win by PSD as a win for USIS. This united reaction was just as exciting to me as the win itself. It set the right tone for the meetings from the start, because the purpose of bringing leaders from all the businesses together is to use all our resources to grow the total business. This reflects back on my last AskRandy message, that we are one team: Team USIS.

Focusing on the Future

The full leadership team from each business made detailed, comprehensive presentations to the entire group on Wednesday and Thursday. On Friday, the senior leaders made briefer, big-picture presentations to representatives from our partners at Welsh, Carson, Anderson & Stowe. All of these presentations demonstrated that our businesses and USIS as a whole are focused firmly on the future.

So many ideas were presented that it would be impossible for me to share them all. However, I would like to discuss three key points that became clear to me over the course of the three days.

First, as I mentioned earlier in this message, I am very impressed with the quality of our leadership teams. We used a similar process to what many large companies use for strategic planning sessions. I can tell you from direct experience that strategic planning participants at large companies, who have gone through these sessions numerous times, could not have done a better job in preparing and presenting than our teams did. Their dedication was exemplary, and I could not be more pleased with the plans we have for our collective future.

Second, we have a strong history of performance and excellent relationships with customers, which is a great foundation for success. However, we must ask ourselves, "Are we leveraging these customer relationships to the full extent? Can we do more in this area to accelerate growth?" As we go forward, we must maximize the business potential of our performance record and customer relationships, which will only happen if we continue to find ways to add value to our customers' businesses.

Finally, as we consider our plans for 2007 and beyond, we must focus and prioritize initiatives for each of our businesses. Many excellent ideas were presented at the planning sessions, but, like all companies, we do not have the capital and human resources to do everything on the list. I have asked each of the three businesses to prioritize and select their top initiatives, with some additional initiatives in reserve if we are successful in implementing the ones with highest priority. These selections will be made based on the projected return on the investment and the potential to fuel growth. We must see a solid return, which to me would be most attractive if the payback on the investment is one year or less.

Although many detailed plans were discussed and developed during the strategy sessions, the strategic growth direction for each business can be summarized in broad terms. ISD must grow capacity and make a significant start in commercial investigations. PSD must build a business development team and fill the pipeline with Requests for Proposals (RFPs). CSD must build a world-class sales team and take a substantial market share.

The prioritization process will set the stage for developing FY2007 operating plans, to be presented in August when the full leadership group will meet again. I will report to you further on the initiatives when the prioritization process is complete. Thanks again for all your support during this first year.

Randy E. Dobbs
CEO

Contact: AskRandy@usis.com

AskRandy #41

Ensuring a Safer Future Today.™

| AskRandy | Number 41 | March 30, 2007 |

TO: All USIS Employees

FROM: Randy Dobbs

When I last communicated with you we had just closed the books on our first quarter. The AskRandy message sent in February discussed the unexpected headwinds we were facing and that we had not achieved our earnings objectives for the first time in my two years as CEO of USIS. That AskRandy message discussed in frank terms how great companies faced realities and reacted to unexpected challenges. Following that message, USIS leaders examined plans in each of our businesses and for the overall company. Their goal was to determine what was working, what wasn't working relative to our 2007 plans, and make appropriate adjustments to improve our FY 2007 performance.

As we start to close the books for the second quarter of FY 2007, I have much better news to report. Each of our businesses is dealing with reality and while we are still facing some of the unexpected headwinds reported earlier, because of decisive actions taken across USIS we are making progress. The remainder of this AskRandy will discuss my insights as we reach the mid-point of our financial year. I will also share thoughts about the future of employee communication efforts across USIS and how the AskRandy message will change to meet your critical information needs.

Business Adjustments Moving USIS Ahead

At the end of the first quarter our leaders reviewed their business plans and made appropriate adjustments to both sustain and improve our ongoing business performance. However, while these immediate adjustments had to be made to recapture our momentum, we did not lose our long-term focus as each of our businesses continued to invest in people and programs that drive our revenue growth. These adjustments impacted less than 1% of our entire workforce and were primarily focused on indirect and support operation costs.

The whole USIS organization did a wonderful job in evaluating and implementing the actions required to recapture momentum. My congratulations go out to all of you! Another high point, which says a great deal about the people of USIS, is that the required actions and necessary changes were well communicated. Each of our business leaders worked hard to dispel rumors. I have always found that "the reality" is never as bad or as dramatic as the rumor mill makes it out to be, and that is why for many months rumors have had less and less of a place at USIS. We are very open and we run all of our businesses that way. I appreciate the work our leaders do to get the straight information out to you as rapidly as possible.

While the second quarter still has some challenges, it will be better than our first quarter performance in both revenue and earnings. It is not exactly as we originally designed it and we will miss our year-to-date earnings objectives because of our first quarter performance, but we will be relatively close to our operating plan for revenue and from an earnings standpoint as well. Overall, this is good news.

1 of 4

The USIS of today is putting the right people in the right jobs, building better and better processes, and experiencing great work force productivity. These are our strengths. The three things we said that we would do – and that we have done well for the past two years – are the strengths we continue to demonstrate today. The one thing we are still not achieving, which is the toughest part of our four business focus areas, is growth. Our biggest issue and challenge remains: We simply aren't getting the new growth we need to really drive our overall performance to higher levels. With that said, I will share some thoughts from my perspective about business successes, adjustments made to put us in the right direction, and what we must accomplish to create the growth this company needs.

ISD Success

We had a huge turnaround in our ISD business in the last 90 days. ISD weathered significant contractual changes to the case closing and review processes that were mandated by federal agencies and our OPM customer. These outside-our-company mandated changes increased administrative time and impacted our ability to realize earnings. To improve overall performance, ISD put processes in place that improved execution. The entire team came together to improve ISD's overall quality of work and case closure capabilities. It was impressive how ISD leadership used the great minds and good ideas of so many people on the team to make huge improvements to productivity, which increased throughout that business, while also tackling initiatives that focused on the quality of work produced.

While ISD was the biggest part of our miss in the first quarter, this business will meet or exceed its operating plan in the second quarter. What a dramatic improvement and my hat is off to all of the ISD team! Your combined emphasis on process and individual performance is paying off in terms of closing cases and the quality of work. I believe this is representative of what ISD has always done. The team faces problems, makes necessary changes to adjust plans and processes, and accomplishes these tasks with a positive, winning attitude. That is why nobody in the security investigations business can outperform us! As ISD is demonstrating once again, they are the biggest and the best in this field and continue to act that way.

PSD Focus

At the end of the second quarter, our PSD business is going to be very close to its operating plan for revenue and earnings because of this business's strong performance in the first quarter. PSD accomplished this primarily through growth of existing contracts, in other words, through organic growth. My congratulations go to PSD for doing a great job in taking advantage of existing contracts and related new business opportunities. The simplest way to grow any business is to satisfy existing customers to the point they award you more work because they have confidence in your business team.

Growing new business opportunities remains the challenge for PSD. The PSD business development team, which has been in place for about nine months, has worked hard to generate an $8 billion sales funnel of potential opportunities within the core capabilities of PSD. However, due to the Iraq war effort and the federal government's Continuing Resolution that has impacted federal agencies and their ability to create additional spending, these new opportunities and business awards have been delayed.

While the PSD team is pursuing every lead that could generate new business growth, the reality is that unless we win new business in the second half of this fiscal year our FY 2007 and FY 2008 earnings objectives will not be realized. The focus must remain on getting new business opportunities and capturing contract re-bids, such as our existing Iraq and ATA contracts. I appreciate all that PSD has accomplished,

AskRandy #41 *continued*

| AskRandy | Number 41 | March 30, 2007 |

and I ask them to continue to push hard in these areas that will have an impact on the business's sustained performance and ability to grow in the coming months.

CSD Efforts

As discussed in the last AskRandy, growing CSD is very important to our future as we work to modify the commercial-to-government mix at USIS. This is critical to assure overall company performance and increasing USIS' ability to grow and sustain our strong financial track record. To support this effort, we made significant investments in CSD over the past year. We added sales and marketing professionals to help us capture the new opportunities that would lead to CSD revenue growing faster than our government businesses.

Unfortunately, CSD missed its first quarter targets, as October and November were solid months but business began to decline in December. That decline in orders from existing customers has continued in the second quarter, which will drive a further business financial miss. Explore is performing well against its plan, and we are moving forward in our insurance business which is one of our biggest segments, but the single largest segment in the CSD business is transportation. While our relationships continue to be strong in the transportation industry, as evidenced by the excellent showing at our annual Transportation Advisory Board meeting, this market has been impacted negatively by economic conditions because the auto industry is down, new home construction is down, and rail/truck shipments are down in total due to this and slower retail inventory rebuild. So, while the overall economy continues to be decent, our CSD business is heavily impacted by these trends.

That said and acknowledged, CSD leadership knows that they can't wait until economic winds change to create additional growth opportunities. As we reach the halfway point of our fiscal year, CSD is facing into its challenges by closely evaluating its entire business plan. The result is that CSD will work to grow more in its other market segments such as health care, retail, and financial services. CSD must shift gears and become less dependent on the trucking and transportation industry in the future, which will be essential to reliable growth. CSD is at the heart of USIS' growth challenge and I appreciate the all hands effort at CSD and the continuing hard work to move us forward in new areas of potential growth opportunity.

Functional Areas and Future Communications

Over the past quarter, our functional teams closely evaluated their plans and made thoughtful adjustments to control costs. I want to express my appreciation for this continuing effort that has already closely examined all USIS functional and support activities and the associated costs of those activities. Because of this effort, we are optimizing our business performance. Our functional teams are still supporting our three businesses and their critical needs in terms of required customer facing and revenue producing projects. This success is due to focused cost control, strong process improvements, and company wide efforts to think and act differently, such as the Bullet Train.

Before I close, I want to briefly return to the importance of good communication. Two years ago when I arrived as CEO of USIS, I began my AskRandy communication. At the time there was no routine divisional or individual business communications. Today, ISD has a great newsletter that is well over a year old and the PSD newsletter is several months old and getting better all the time. These are fabulous, employee-directed communications. CSD, which because of its more centralized nature has mainly used face-to-face communications in the past, is now also beginning a newsletter. The first issue will be out in early May.

AskRandy   Number 41   March 30, 2007

Because this individual business-focused communication effort is now a reality, I am going to send AskRandy to you once a quarter. This will be the CEO's perspective about the business and what happened during the quarter, as well as new information about where we are directing our efforts for the upcoming quarter. The emphasis, as well as the timing, will be different than what we have been doing but should create an even stronger communication environment at USIS. Look to see the next AskRandy in early July.

The USIS way!

In summary, USIS is moving ahead and the second quarter is an improvement over the first quarter. It wasn't how we originally planned it, but that is what this team has always been very good at: looking realistically at our progress, making appropriate plans based on these realities, and seizing new opportunities to help address areas where we have issues. Over the past quarter, our ISD team worked hard and successfully overcame many of its challenges. This in turn helped us cover some of our shortfalls as CSD re-tooled to face the market realities impacting its performance. Our functional teams also pitched in to help us control our costs.

This is the mark of a great team! In my last AskRandy I noted that the best team wins and not necessarily the best strategy. What I think makes this a great team, and what is exciting about being part of USIS, is that we work together to optimize what is going well and use our wins to offset areas where we are experiencing some problems. We then take corrective actions where we are facing those challenges which helps us continue to drive stronger overall performance. That is how USIS faces reality. While the reality of any business is that there will be ups and downs in specific areas or markets, not every business can or will act this way, work together, and produce better results. This collaborative effort is what sets us apart. That is what makes us a unique company, and I am proud to be a part of this high performing team.

Randy E. Dobbs

CEO

Contact: AskRandy@usis.com

2007 USIS Veteran's Day Message

AskRandy   Number 47   November 9, 2007

TO: All USIS Employees

FROM: Randy Dobbs

This weekend, Americans across our great nation will observe Veterans Day. Americans will view and march in parades, veterans organizations will arrange special events, and volunteers and workers at national cemeteries will place American flags on the graves of those who served, many of whom made the final sacrifice to keep this nation free. Therefore, I hope each of you will join me in taking a moment to remember the great and personal sacrifice that many Americans made to ensure our freedom. I also hope you will join me in thanking those who have served or who are serving in the armed services of this great nation.

As you may know, November 11 is the anniversary of the day in 1918 that the armistice was signed in the Forest of Compiègne by the Allies and the Germans that ended World War I. Originally known as Armistice Day, it was changed to Veterans Day by an Act of Congress in 1954. At that time, President Eisenhower called on citizens to observe the day by remembering the sacrifices of all those who fought so gallantly for this nation.

World War I seems like ancient history to many Americans. Indeed, many of the families who will display our country's flag from their homes this year – honoring veterans and the service people who are serving this nation today – weren't even born in 1954 when Armistice Day became Veterans Day. However, my point is that this weekend is a time to remember not only our debt of gratitude to men and women in the service, both past and present, of our country, but to also remember that each of us has a continuing role to play in the hard work that ensures this nation remains strong and free. It is a time to remember that we honor those who serve by being active and concerned citizens in this great country.

In that regard, I am proud of our special efforts on behalf of our nation. Our critical national security efforts help preserve the liberties and values we collectively hold dear. As I visit USIS employees in each of our businesses across the United States, I am inspired by your hard work and great accomplishments. That makes me think of how lucky I am to be part of such a great team. So, on this commemoration of those who have shepherded our nation's safety to this point, I thank each of you for the great work you do on behalf of our fellow citizens and our nation.

Randy E. Dobbs
CEO
Contact: AskRandy@usis.com

AskRandy is an official internal publication of USIS, which is responsible for its contents. AskRandy is intended solely for communication of timely corporate and business information from the CEO to USIS employees. This publication is not intended for external release. Any other use of this internal publication should be coordinated with USIS Corporate Communication at michael.john@usis.com.

USIS 100-day Plan Before Officially Becoming CEO, January-February 2005

Randy Dobbs
January and February 2005

First 100-Days – Suggested Actions

Look and listen:

- Start the dialog with employees and managers:
- Individual meetings with executives
- Management meetings
- Town halls
- Breakfast/lunch with the CEO (10 to 12 employees at a time)

Review of business plans (co.-wide and divisional), objectives and expected results.

Review of infrastructure:

- What's in place
- What do we need

Meet the customers.

Hitting the road:

- Start with Fairfax, PBU (DC Suburb), Western PA, Tulsa – these are biggest employee and management concentrations
- ISD – Each business unit: Eastern, Southern, Central, Mountain, Western
- CSD – Florida and Montana

Analyze the data

- Changes to current direction?
- Employee communication needs
- (Re)Organization – first phase
- Customer communications
- Infrastructure priorities

Develop a Plan. Communicate, communicate, communicate!

Organizational Observations

Company-Wide

- Command and control culture.
- Not nearly enough communication from the top.
- No vision of next step.
- Infrastructure is a framework only. No real systems, SOP's etc. No standard methods of reporting, at least on the non-finance side.
- <u>Finance</u> function most mature of infrastructure depts. <u>HR</u> still working on systems and processes. Strong site support function. Services (compensation, benefits, HR systems, organization development) needs to be strengthened. <u>IT</u> function basically non-existent. <u>Marketing</u> function seems scattered and not too effective.
- Paternalistic, controlling culture has to go. But need to educate managers how to deal with new world.

ISD

- Phil Harper is really running the Division.
- Pete is a short-timer, good first lieutenant. He does what Phil tells him to do.
- Paternalistic culture is strongest here.
- Weak second-line management.
- District Managers are backbone of organization and should be the target of more communications.
- BUD's are workload managers, not people nor business managers.
- Need leadership and management training at all levels.
- Relationship with customer seems to have problems.
- Management knows we need to diversify base of business, not sure how.

PSD

- Acting Division President. Need to anoint or bring in new person pretty soon.
- Strained environment from last Division President. Lots of volatile personalities. Harsh communication style.
- All over the place on the business front. Very opportunistic. Maybe this is OK.
- Business unit leaders all ex-govies. No real business experience. They are good program managers, however.
- Management training desperately needed at all levels.

CSD

- Jim Collins good sales person, very enthusiastic. Not a good people manager or operations manager.
- See selves as different from rest of business and they are. However, the people issues are, of course, very similar.
- Very strong HR leadership in Division. A good place to pilot programs.

USIS 100-day Plan After 30 days on the Job, March 2005

New CEO
1st 100 Days +

- Investigations Services Division
- Go on a listening tour to the mine and the field to hear what's on the minds of ISD directors, local managers and employees. When visiting the field, meet with local management and groups of investigators.
- Visit with OPM and OS (will need a different security clearance for this customer) customers to find out what's on their mind
- Add better operational analytics to assist in improving the agility of market and other forces that affect the business. This business moves to slow to changes that occur (market, customer, regulatory, employee, et al).
- Start to look at how information technology could enhance ISD business processes. ISD seems very manually driven and what you may hear from ISD will point the finger at OPM. OPM can't restrict all of the processes we do that could be more automated and where they do, begin a win/win relationship with them to at least discuss using technology to enhance production and quality.
- Very autocratically run business. Begin to analyze how to empower VPs, directors, managers and employees to add more value.
- Align compensation (Field investigator pay, District Manager pay, VP/Director pay, incentives et al) with what's important to the organization.
- Review operational processes. Conduct a business review with ISD leaders to see what can be done to improve case production (this is strong and getting stronger but could always use a fresh look) and overall efficiency . Consider a business process reengineering effort to get ideas on how to improve operational efficiency and other process improvements within ISD.
- Develop better talent development to increase the strength of the management team
- ISD is full of workload managers vs. business managers (senior and junior). Take a look at this dynamic and begin to consider how to develop the ISD management team into a more business management orientation.
- Give managers authority to make decisions and trust in the brainpower that we have hired and developed. Then, in return for this autonomy, hold managers accountable for their business decisions (this seems particularly acute in ISD's field organization).
- Add business oversight to this Division to better manage profitable growth
- Review organizational design
- Evaluate people

Professional Services Division

- Initiate PSD President search
- Visit with ex-PSD President (Tony Gallo –lives in Falls Church, VA) to get his views on the business, people, challenges, et al
- Go on a listening tour to key PSD locations to hear what's on the minds of PSD VPs, directors, managers and employees.

- Evaluate Protective Services & Training business as a viable long-term focus for PSD
- Visit with large customers to find out what's on their mind
- Develop better talent development to increase the strength of the management team (PS&T business specifically seems to be overly mission oriented and not business oriented, consider how to address this).
- Work with interim PSD President and Corporate HR to eliminate the dysfunctionality within the division
- Add business oversight to this Division to better manage profitable growth
- Review organizational design
- Evaluate people

Commercial Services Division

- Visit with large customers to find out what's on their mind
- Go on a listening tour of CSD locations (employees are primarily in Tulsa) to hear what's on the minds of CSD VPs, directors, managers and employees.
- President is very sales driven which is good but needs mentoring to become more "Presidential" as well as how best to deal with operations, technology, people, and growth issues. Consider how best to assist.
- Oftentimes decisions are made without a thorough analysis and business case rationale, add more rigor to the decision making process.
- Work with President to review IT infrastructure and platform design to make sure we are using our IT platforms and IT assets in the best way. Personally, I would hire a CIO to lead this effort (see corporate comments below).
- Consider an overall strategic and operational review to make sure CSD is structured properly, addressing the right things relative to their growth and to ensure the core issues relative to the overall business are brought to the table. Consider an outside resource.
- Add business oversight to this Division to better manage profitable growth
- Review organizational design
- Evaluate people

Corporate

- Review corporate infrastructure to see what is needed to add more value to the divisions and position USIS to be a public company (i.e. IT, Legal, Corporate Development). Look hard at why we don't have a CIO or a General Counsel.
- Review Corporate Development function as it seems unorganized and not terribly effective – find out what they do and how they add value (i.e. bottom line profits) to the divisions.
- Decide on where the Corporate HQ is going to be and if there is a going to be a move, begin to discuss all the ramifications of this.
- Review Western PA space planning and consider whether it's effective and how it can be improved.
- Consider developing a corporate marketing/external communications effort to better communicate who USIS is to the marketplace.

- Develop a more traditional performance review and appraisal process and align with what's important to the division/function/organization.
- Review organizational design
- Evaluate people

USIS overall

- Re-establish a connection with the employees. Build pride in the name of US Investigations Services. Recognize and celebrate all the good that our Company does for its Customers, Employees and National Security.
- Understand that leadership is lacking in the organization. Make leadership a central focus of your management objectives and the division presidents' objectives.
- Improve communication throughout the organization. Small things matter to the masses. Quarterly performance reports and/or, 'State of the Company' reports via website or some other means (biweekly e-mails?). Take a look at who's on e-mail and who's not and understand why.
- Increase the speed of things. When decisions are made to implement a course of action, get people to get to it. (This is particularly true in ISD but recently something to look at across all of USIS.)
- Listen to the ideas that percolate up. Some could be impractical and/or off point, but they will indicate what people think needs to be fixed and what's on their minds.
- Embrace the help of experts and consultants. Encourage the division presidents to use outside expertise in solving complex business problems.
- Consider visiting with former, retired USIS senior executives — Phil Gasiewicz (former COO – lives in Grove City, PA) and O.B. Seaton (former EVP and PSD and CSD Group President - lives in Denver, CO). This would only take a couple of hours and could be of assistance in understanding their experiences at USIS and their perspective.

Mid-term items

- Consider a rigorous strategic planning process
- Consider a much more structured succession planning process both at the Corporate-level as well as the Divisional level.
- Update USIS policies and procedures to reflect a more open, accessible corporate image and move away form the old government influences on our culture.
- We are a service business and, as you know, people drive service businesses. Instill a people driven business model and a dynamic work environment that empowers our employees and managers to make a difference and add value (customer, bottom-line et al). Happy people —happy customers—happy investors.

New Manager Assimilation Questions and Responses

I discussed the New Manager Assimilation process at the end of chapter 7. Here are the four questions again and some of the responses I've received in various positions throughout my career.

1) What do you know about Randy Dobbs?

He's tall. He's a golfer. He drives a Corvette. He's married and has kids. He likes to-do lists. He's intense. He's open. He's upfront with people. He's detailed. He has the courage of his convictions. He's a good delegator. We haven't heard anything negative about him yet.

2) What do you want to know about Randy Dobbs?

What's your management style? Why did you take this job? What training have you had for it? What are you career goals? Tell us more about your family. How long will you be here? Are you empowering? What do you know about us? How will you help us? What do you do outside of GE? Do you have any P&L experience? What are your pet peeves?

3) What should Randy know about you?

Our styles. What we didn't like about the previous leader. Our priorities. Our career goals. You should learn about us individually, first-hand and not by hearsay. You should find out if we want to be here. We have an uncertainty about the future. We want to know what it's going to take to succeed.

4) What are the problems/issues that face our organization and face us as a team?

Lawsuits. History of poor performance. Lack of systems. Lack of processes. Lack of training. Lack of career planning. The office facilities stink. Other organizations within our company are out of control. Poor morale. We don't have enough people. Lack of communication. Pay inequities. Too much paperwork versus technology. Too time-constrained. Too many meetings. No long-range planning.

Change and Growth Monster Slides

These slides are from my presentation at the FY 2008 USIS Leadership Conference, my third conference as CEO. The first slide is a takeoff on the original change monster slide presented at the FY 2006 conference, while the second slide, including caricatures of me and Senior VP for Corporate Development Phil Sweeney, depicts the new growth monster of the company's future.

What About Yesterday's Change Monster?

Yesterday's
Gone

 Introducing... Tomorrow's Monster at USIS

The two-headed growth monster... looking for growth aliens

USIS Shared Values Posters

Vision

To be the premier provider of knowledge-based security solutions, ensuring a safer future today.

Mission

To deliver best-in-class people, processes, and technology in partnership with our diverse customer base, creating value for shareholders, employees, and community.

INSIGHT
INTELLIGENCE
INTEGRITY

Key Strategies:

Integrity: *Establish a USIS culture of unconditional daily compliance.*

People: *Inspire and motivate everyone to become the best they can be; reward success and excellence.*

Process: *Create a business culture that constantly challenges the status quo to find smarter, more efficient ways of working.*

Growth: *Make sustained, profitable growth the lifeblood of the business through a relentless focus on value-added customer solutions.*

Customer: *Deliver value-added solutions that enhance the success of our clients in serving their customers and achieving their missions.*

Community: *Make a difference where we live as well as work; be a recognized partner in the community.*

USIS
INSIGHT
INTELLIGENCE
INTEGRITY

Selected Slides from USIS FY 2008
Leadership Conference, October 2007

 Thinking About Tomorrow...

♦ **Amazing how things change**

YESTERDAY USIS	TODAY USIS
Little Communication	Ask Randy, Town Halls, Division Newsletters, Local Business Ownership
Minimal Career Development	Performance Appraisal, Meritocracy, Career Planning, Open House, Professional Development
Limited Business Metrics	Quarterly Business Reviews, Monthly Business Ops Reviews, Annual Budget Reviews, Annual Strategy Sessions, Strong Financial Metrics
Strong Revenue Growth	Acquired Explore, Eliminated ISD Backlog, Developed Iraq Opportunity, **Missed Growth Objectives '06 & '07**

Growth in '08 Mandatory!

 USIS Leadership Focused on Winning

♦ **People**
- Organizational integration
- New Leadership Team
- Many internal promotions
- Critical new talent added
- Focused on training
- Dealing with poor performers

♦ **Productivity**
- Budgets
- Bullet Trains
- Metrics
- Compensation
- Sourcing
- Productivity Deck

♦ **Process**
- Metrics/reporting
- Unique IT actions
- Proposals
- Bullet Trains/Productivity Deck
- Process mapping/compliance
- Production calls

Our 4 Plays
People, Process, Productivity & Growth

The "Red Zone"

♦ **Growth**
- New offerings
- Organic Growth
- New business development focus
- FY06 Revenue - Up 5%
- FY06 EBITDA - Up 33%

FY07 Leadership Conference Growth Plan

We even discussed growth as a critical element of future investment

 My Five Personal Actions That Improve My Growth Leadership

◆ 1. People are People not Human Resources

- Living/Breathing/Imperfect…Who Enliven/Excite/ Disappoint you
- I/You have profound impact on them as leaders for growth

◆ 2. Be Strong in Our Growth Focus

- Experts say we only use about 10% of our Brains
- Not sure but I believe we only use 10% of the Full Strength of our Company
- I/You have to be strong enough to Pull the Strengths out of the People We Lead

My Five Personal Actions That Improve My Growth Leadership

◆ 3. Plan…and Improve
- By all means have Goals & Strategies
- But I/You need to be willing to Improve & Grow by:
  - Just saying Yes sometimes
  - Making Mistakes
  - Pay Attention
  - Start Anywhere
  - Enjoy the Ride

◆ 4. I can't do this Alone
- Organizational Pyramid is Ancient & Transforming
- I/You need to be on the Level of People We Lead…Not above them

 My Five Personal Actions That Improve My Growth Leadership

◆ 5. Grow Now! (Live the Now!)
- This is the Moment
- Don't wait for some Promotion/Milestone to make you Focus on Growth/Feel Alive
- It is Never too Early/It is Never too Late
- Remember You only have Moments to Live

I can Drive Growth by Focusing on my Strengths and NOT Worrying about my Weaknesses!

Selected Slides from Philips Medical Systems N.A.
and Services Reorganization Presentation, April 2003

PHILIPS

Challenges We Face

- Siloed organizational structure
- Poor functional alignment
- Extensive management structure
- Poor Business Line relationships
- Selling expenses high to industry norms
- Missing direct opportunities in geographies
- Lack of fundamental processes, roles and responsibilities... for business that has grown 5X
- Lack of strategic roadmap and communication

2

PHILIPS

SSR NA Mission/Goals

A renewed SSR organization focused on exceeding our financial targets, while increasing customer and employee satisfaction

- Exceed Financial Metrics
- Geographically aligned Sales and Service... staffed by the best people
- Best In Class cost and productivity
- Common core processes and metrics
- Unparalleled customer satisfaction
- Improved employee retention and satisfaction

3

PHILIPS

SSR NA Accomplishments to Date

- Defined new SSR NA organizational structure
  - Single Sales organization for Full-Line, U/S, NM
  - Supply Chain consolidated into Service
  - Marketing integrated into Sales with elevated BL/SSR relationships
- Aligned Sales and Service Zones and Regions
  - Shifted the structure to INCREASE customer-facing positions
- Developed cost reduction plan - $36.8M
  - Sales: $17.7M (Impacts 200 + heads....
  - Service: $19.1M   details to follow)
- Created 5th Zone in US...eliminated large dealer territory
- Redesign of processes and development of implementation plan

4

Selected Slides from Philips Medical Systems N.A. Bullet Train Presentation, August 2003

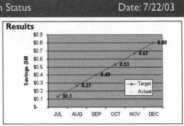

PHILIPS　　　　Bullet Train Status　　　　Date: 7/22/03

Bullet Train: Telecom

Objective: Reduce SSR 2nd Half 2003 Telecom spending by 13%

Owner: Randall Gifford

Team: David Wither – Corp. Telecom
Tim Mahanna – Service
Hank Wysong – Communications Mgr.
Dan Lawrence – PDS
Todd Wells – Black Belt

Target($ Saving 2003): $0.5 M

Results

Risk Mitigation

Risk
- Negative impact to field from 4th quarter voice mail consolidation (lost voice mails, new numbers, etc.)
- PDS 800# optimization may impact dial in ability if local access is not available in all areas

Mitigation Plan
- Streamline transition period (over a weekend), convert as many numbers as possible, communicate transition broadly.
- Analyzing usage data to understand optimum course of action to maximize savings and minimize field impact

Focusing on identifying savings opportunities

Philips Medical Systems, R. Dobbs, 26/8/03　　2

PHILIPS

Bullet Train Status
Date: 8-21-03

Bullet Train: "Freight"

Objective: To reduce all freight cost in second half 2003.
(Service and non service freight)

Owner: Steve Kellett

Team: Ron Robey, Jim Travis, Richard Conner, Bob Egiziano, Payton Patterson

Destination($ Saving 2003):

Non Service Freight (Gifford)   **$0.5M**

Service/Equipment Freight (Kellett)   **$0.5M**

Results

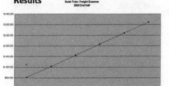

Plan

Actions	Group (Ser./non ser)	Owner	Target $	Impact Date	Actual $	Plan YE $	Gap $	2004 Rollover	Status
Restrict Overnight Service (non-parts)	Non	Kellett	$0.100	7-31	$0.0	$0.100			
Restrict "Next Flight Out" and "Drive" (Target 60% reduction)	Service	Robey	$0.460	7-31	$0.0	$0.460			
FedEx usage reduction (Target 40% reduction)	Non	Kellett	$0.175	7-31	$0.0	$0.175			
Hold and Call - Priority to Standard	Service	Egiziano	$0.060	7-11	$0.0	$0.060			
Approval for Air Shipment of Systems (Target 10% reduction)	SC	Gifford	$0.180	7-24	$0.0	$0.180			
Consolidation of accounts	Service/Non	Travis	0.045	7-31	$0.0	$0.045			
Total			**$1.020**			**$ 1.020**			

Notes

Account Consolidation

-96 (out of 160) accounts submitted for deletion.

(87 deleted – 3 with remaining balances to be settled)

-9 new accounts requested (1 for each of Dobbs staff)

-Remainder of accounts (less Memphis and Bothell traffic) will be deleted once new accounts numbers are communicated.

-Target >15 total accounts for SSRNA by September 5.

-Proceeding carefully to avoid disruption to service parts distribution.

> *A road map for $1M savings in freight expense for 2003.*

PHILIPS

Bullet Train Status
Date: 8-11-03

Bullet Train: "MARCOM"

Objective: Reduce expenses in Trade shows and Marketing functions during second half

Owner: Randy Rountree

Team: Robinson, Mixon
Harber, July, Biltz

Destination($ Saving 2003): **$1.0 M**

2nd Half Marcom Expense
Results

Plan

Actions	Owner	Target $	Impact Date	Actual $	Plan YE $	Gap $	2004 Rollover	Status
Reduce / Cancel Trade Show	Robinson	$0.42	8/1/03	$0.0	$0.0	$0.0	$0.0	
Reduce Sales Lit. Purchases	Robinson	$0.31	8/1/03	$0.0	$0.0	$0.0	$0.0	
Misc Reductions - Sponsorships	Mixon	$0.13	8/1/03	$0.0	$0.0	$0.0	$0.0	
Reduce / Cancel Bil. Exhibits	Robinson	$0.05	8/1/03	$0.0	$0.0	$0.0	$0.0	
Reduce Spend RSNA Event	Harber	$0.11	8/1/03	$0.0	$0.0	$0.0	$0.0	
Total		**$1.01**			**$0.0**	**$0.0**	**$0.0**	

Comments

- Under target by $43K
- Confirmed cancellation of shows and publications (Starting in August Marketvision is only available online)
- Tracking list of shows for remainder of year and anticipated savings from cancellation or reduction
- There is some risk in the purchase of sales literature from Europe due to the high shipping costs and timeliness of the information

> *A Path to $1.0 million – at Target*

PHILIPS

Bullet Train Status

Date: 8-21-03

Bullet Train: "Corporate Meetings"

Objective: Reduce meeting expenses by limiting and/or reducing corporate meetings

Owner: Randy Rountree

Team: Robinson, Mixon, Criss
Harber, Travis

Destination($ Saving 2003): $0.45M

Results

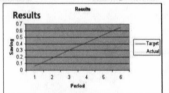

Plan

Actions	Owner	Target $	Impact Date	Actual $	Plan YE $	Gap $	2004 Rollover	Status
Reduce Clin Ed Meetings	Robinson	$ 0.26	12/31/03	$0.0	$0.0	$0.0	$0.0	
Reduce BLU Meetings	Criss	$ 0.10	12/31/03	$0.0	$0.0	$0.0	$0.0	
Reduce Field Sales Meetings	Mixon	$ 0.05	12/31/03	$0.0	$0.0	$0.0	$0.0	
Reduce Exec/ Other Meetings	Harber	$ 0.05	12/31/03	$0.0	$0.0	$0.0	$0.0	
Note: Orginally targeted $250k for Genico included in the Service T&E Target								
Total		**$ 0.46**			**$0.0**	**$0.0**	**$0.0**	

Notes

Currently under expense reduction targets by $210K.

National Sales Meeting scheduled after targets set – risk to target of $300K.

A Path to $450k – at Target

Philips Medical Systems, R. Dobbs, 26/8/03

5

PHILIPS

Bullet Train Status

Date: Aug. 21, 2003

Bullet Train: Temps/consultants (3rd party)

Objective: Reduce the cost of temporary and consultant (including 3rd party vendors) headcount for SSR NA.

* July - Dec, 2003 forecast is $4.64M (target reduction of 31.3%)

Owner: Mark Mindell
Team: Mark Mindell, Ginny Eagle, Chris Richardson, Bill Brager, Roger Biltz, and Ketan Shah

Target ($ Saving 2003): $1.45M

Results

Plan

Actions	Owner	Target $	Impact Date	Actual $	Plan YE $	Gap $	2004 Rollover	Status
1. All current temps, consultants, and 3rd party contractors terminated	Mindell	$1,450,000	08-01-03					
2. Continuance of the above parties after July 31, 2003 must be approved by Mark Mindell	Mindell		07-31-03					
3. Establish a process of new hires of temps/consultants, and centralize their approval by Mark Mindell	Mindell		08-04-03					
4. Where a temp is required try to convert the slot into FTE. This must be approved by Mark Mindell	Mindell		Various					
5. Process for consultants complete by 8/1/03	Mindell		08-04-03					Complete
6. Reduce the SSR consultant budget by 68% (see Ketan's analysis)	Scweringer							
Total		**$1,450,000**			**$**			

Wins/Need Improvements

* A name by name analysis for all SSR temps is complete and accurate.
* Have identified actual end dates for the temps resulting in a more accurate 2nd half projection.
* Reduce the remaining temp force by 50% by the end of August, excluding the CMS Integrated Client temps.
* BB and HR Team working on developing a policy and procedure for temps.
  - Temp process map is complete.

This is a stretch goal, but attainable!

Philips Medical Systems, R. Dobbs, 26/8/03

6

PHILIPS

Example Bullet Train Actions

- T&E
  - Reduced budgets by 40%
  - Reinforced policies on advance booking, lowest fare, etc.
  - Revised GELCO category limits to flag top 5-10%
- Telecom
  - Set $150/mo. limit on cell phone reimbursement
  - Cut off reimbursement of cell phones not approved through Corporate phone process
  - Mandated reservation-less conference calling
- Freight
  - FedEx: default from Next Day Priority to 2nd Day
  - Consolidated FedEx accounts from 160 to 15
- Operating/Office Supplies
  - Cut off multiple ways to buy computer equipment
  - Redeploying PCs...expect no purchases for rest of '03
  - Revamped Office Supply web-site to eliminate non-contract items

Philips Medical Systems, R. Dobbs, 26/8/03   11

Selected Slides from Philips Medical Systems N.A. Board of Management Presentation, November 2004

PHILIPS

Medical Systems – SSR NA Financial Results
($ Millions)

	2002* Actual	2003 Actual	2004 FC	2005** AOP
Sales	3,016	3,148	3,308	3,548
Income from Operations	228	192	270	302
Cash Flow before Financing	273	275	274	314
EPR	226	180	262	295
NOC	149	66	62	50
Employees	6,075	5,318	5,438	5,556

*Best Data Available
**Includes Expected Transfer Price

Dobbs Board of Management, November, 2004

PHILIPS

Medical Systems SSR NA –
Performance Indicators

	2002 Actual	2003 Actual	2004 FC	2005 AOP
Days Sales O/S	50	39	33	33
Days Payable O/S	9	8	8	8
Inventory % of Sales	10.8	7	6.8	5.9
Working Capital Turns	14.9	19.7	53.2	61.1
NOC Turns	4.3	21.7	63.5	74

Dobbs Board of Management, November, 2004

PHILIPS

PMSNA Technology Accomplishments

- ERP System Consolidations – from 6 down to 3 ... moving to 2

- Business Process Automation and Enhancement (SOLAAR)
    - INtelliSIGHT Digital Dashboard
    - RADAR Personalized Data Reporting
    - Order Management Tools
    - Master Data Management
    - Service Contracts Tools
    - Installation Scheduling
    - Pre-trip Approval
    - PTO Approval

- Management of Applicant Pool
    - PeopleClick (Online Recruiting)
    - Automated Requisition and Approval Process

Dobbs Board of Management, November, 2004

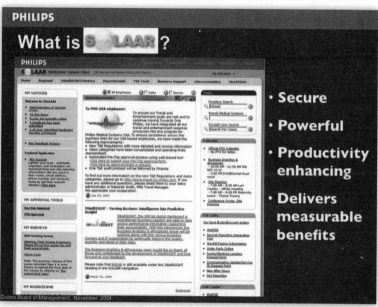

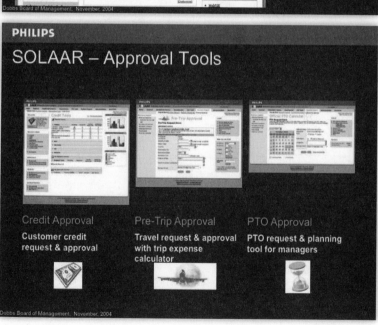

Randy Dobbs 4-Block Chart

Randy Dobbs

Strengths

- Driven, competitive, results-focused leader
- Excellent communicator...can energize a large organization
- Upbeat, enthusiastic....leads with passion
- Strong operational/execution skills... demonstrated success in fix-it situations
- Strong analytical skills...finds basic issues and resolves quickly
- Effective coach/mentor...builds strong, empowered teams

Experience ...... Last 3 Years

- Proactive, strategic/tactical leadership in radically changing Govt/commercial environment
- Provided business leadership to drive organic growth, tough productivity initiatives, a strategic acquisition and overhaul business processes
- Established business communications to inform, educate and build a team of 7,000 associates across North America
- Created new growth initiatives and business development initiatives to both grow and increase brand awareness

Performance.... Last 3 Years

- Successful transition from large company CEO to private equity CEO
- Established new business culture, new senior leadership team and clear operating objectives in four critical areas: people/process/productivity & growth
- Drove revenue CAGR 18% & EBITDA CAGR 27% over 3 year period
- Successful transaction of selling of private company to new financial sponsor for $1.5B / 10.3 x EBITDA

Desires for Next Role

- Ability to leverage experiences & business skills into a broader operating leadership role
- Utilize experiences and working knowledge gained in private equity environment to broaden relationship & opportunities in this environment
- Portfolio CEO/ Operating Partner/ Director are all roles that stand alone or combined attract me as next assignments